A WORLD OF

Sylvie Dare was born in G   to an English mother and a Czech father but has no memory of her parents, Marjorie and Gustave.

A World of Fallen Pieces is her first book and was driven by a deep desire to know them and to discover what happened. Borne out by a vast collection of personal letters, photographs, public records and recorded interviews with family, friends, business associates and a fellow prisoner, a story unfolds which many would find hard to believe. It is a true story.

Though her early life was spent in Paris, she grew up in England. When the Home Office granted her British Nationality at age eighteen, they warned her that it would be dangerous to return to her birthplace, by then under Communist control.

Sylvie devoted much of her working life to the development of young people through training and enterprise and has held a number of directorships in the public and private sector. In 1990 she was made a Fellow of the Chartered Management Institute. She still acts as a school governor and Business Adviser for the Prince's Trust. She lives in Somerset with her husband of 56 years. They have four grown up children, ten grandchildren and one great-grandson.

A World Of

Fallen Pieces

A true story of Love, Peace and War

Sylvie Dare

Copyright © 2018 Sylvie Dare

ISBN: 978-0-244-13066-4

All rights reserved, including the right to reproduce this book, or portions thereof in any form. No part of this text may be reproduced, transmitted, downloaded, decompiled, reverse engineered, or stored, in any form or introduced into any information storage and retrieval system, in any form or by any means, whether electronic or mechanical without the express written permission of the author.

This is a true story and the names of the characters are real.

The letters from Gustave to Marjorie, except where otherwise stated, are transcribed from handwritten originals in English but the ones he wrote whilst interned are translated into English from the originals handwritten in German. The same applies to the letters to Gustave from his employers Ginzkey and those written by Graham from his FLAK posting (p.143-5).

The moral rights of the author have been asserted.

A CIP catalogue record of this book is available from the British Library.

Set in Garamond

Front Cover Design: Riordan Sailes – great grandson of Marjorie and Gustave

PublishNation
www.publishnation.co.uk

For Andrew, Maria, Emma and Sean

for their children...and for theirs

and for ALL my wider family
Presently in England, Wales, France, Austria, Germany,
America, Australia, Africa, and Cambodia

So they need never forget

Acknowledgements

To my late brother Graham Lange for so faithfully keeping the wealth of records, without which this book could not have been written, but also for his permission to use four of the chapters in his memoir: *From Shades of Night*, privately printed, 2007.

My heartfelt thanks to:
Maureen Lange, my sister-in-law, researcher, encourager, sounding board, and Guardian Angel for her patience, understanding and positivity.

Sarah Young, my editor for her hard work, for sticking with me and for keeping faith.

Clive Williams OBE, for his invaluable guidance.

My darling John, my husband of 56 years for his love and support and his hours of solitude throughout this project.

Jean, Ross, Karen and Rita for sharing the journey and spurring me on.

Conventions

The Names – It is no accident that the names of people and places turn up either with different spellings or in different forms. Place names have been changed as new boundaries have been formed. Personal "given" names change, sometimes by personal preference, from one country to another. Adopted nicknames appear in letters and some names are lost in translation.

Given Name	*French adopted*	*Nickname*
Gustav	Gustave	Gustl
Graham		Gustl
James		Jimmy
Sylvia	Sylvie	

(Sylva Langlova: Czech (Le Monde)

Sudetenland, Czechoslovakia:
Formerly –	Bohemia, Austria-Hungary
German Bohemia –	for a short period after WWI as part of the Austrian/German Republic
Germany –	from 1938 to 1945
Czechoslovakia –	from Aug 1945 to Oct 1993
Czech Republic –	from 1 Oct 1993 to present

Reichenberg is the German name for Liberec
Maffersdorf is the German name for Vratislavice
Since the expulsion of the Germans in 1946 the latter names are more widely used

The Letters – throughout the book, the extracts from letters have been copied verbatim and for the sake of accuracy, no corrections have been made to the text where the grammar has been lost in translation.

CONTENTS

Foreword		1
Chapter 1	The Flight to Prague	5
Chapter 2	From Drudgery to Dance	12
Chapter 3	A new life in Paris	21
Chapter 4	Romance arrives with Gustave	31
Chapter 5	Maffersdorf, Reichenberg	42
Chapter 6	Anna and Josef	48
Chapter 7	Baby Graham	56
Chapter 8	Separation before Marriage	68
Chapter 9	Paris and the Depression	82
Chapter 10	Severn Beach or Riva Bella?	87
Chapter 11	War clouds…the Foreign Legion	93
Chapter 12	Uprooted - Camps to Maffersdorf	99
Chapter 13	Hitler Youth and Gestapo Threats	110
Chapter 14	Hinzert Concentration Camp	117
Chapter 15	Gliding into Conscription	138
Chapter 16	Escaping Dresden to Baby Sister	144
Chapter 17	Saved from Execution by a PoW	159
Chapter 18	Following Graham to Paris	170
Chapter 19	An English welcome turns sour	181
Chapter 20	Her Ladyship's Tutor	193

Chapter 21	No Visa for Christmas	204
Chapter 22	Prague Airspace 5 March 1946	212
Chapter 23	Eyewitness Accounts	214
Chapter 24	All at Sea with the News	217
Afterword	**The Author's Voice**	225
	A Tribute to *The Beach*	230
	First Source of Discovery	235
	Back to my Birthplace	238
	The Man who saved my Life	239
	Author's Insights	244
	The Unmarried Mother	246
	Expulsion of the Germans from Czechoslovakia	248
	SS Special Concentration Camp Hinzert	249
	Peter Hassall & Maurice Gould	251
	On a Lighter Note: Lucerne	254
	And so, in Conclusion	256

APPENDICES	260
Bibliography	277
Primary Sources	278
Footnote Sources	280
Disclaimer: And more about Ginzkey	281

FOREWORD

A World of Fallen Pieces is a biographical history of an Anglo-German relationship during wartime. It is the true story of the love between Marjorie, an Englishwoman, and Gustave, a Sudeten German. Their relationship develops against a backdrop of increasing political unrest, surviving World War II against seemingly impossible odds. I am their daughter and am indebted to my brother Graham Lange for preserving the correspondence on which much of this book is based.

The narrative is factual, based on sources contained in family archives and interviews with witnesses, but in order to complete the jigsaw, I have occasionally augmented our research with imagination.

It started with a box of letters found among some items bequeathed to me by my Aunt. Intrigued, I brought the box home but it was several weeks before I ventured to open it; when I did, thankfully I was not alone. I had decided to share the find with my daughter Maria, just eighteen at the time, and what we read shook us to the core.

Earnest and full of fear, the letters dated late 1945 and early 1946 were written by Marjorie to her sister. Among them was a lengthy translation giving a detailed account of what happened. Its contents led me on a very long search to find out more. Maureen, my dear sister in law, was my encouragement to write the book and she became my treasured researcher. Each discovery led to another and as uncomfortable silences were broken, more letters and documents were brought to light. Our search led us to Austria, Germany, Switzerland, France, Czechoslovakia during the Cold War, Jersey and as far away as Canada.

Graham was key to our research and he forms a large part of the story. He wrote his own biography, *From Shades of Night*, which was privately printed. With his permission, I have used excerpts from this to provide the most accurate account of his *great escape (ch15-18)*. Bit by bit over almost two decades, it became a labour of love and the following story unfolded.

The love that I have is Yours

CHAPTER ONE

THE FLIGHT TO PRAGUE

Tuesday 5 March 1946
Air France office, Rue Lafayette

Gustave was still talking to the officials at the Air France desk. Whatever was holding things up now? Marjorie craned her neck to try to work out what was being said. After all they had been through, surely they wouldn't keep him behind and make her fly alone with the baby? At eighteen months, she was really quite a handful.

Shushing and jiggling the fretful child, Marjorie tried to quell her rising panic. A young Frenchman behind her shifted his feet; the queue was becoming restless. Oh, what could possibly be the problem now? She couldn't see her husband's expression but watched the officials feverishly, trying to catch someone's eye. There appeared to be some hold up with Gustave's papers.

After yet more delay and protracted discussion Gustave was ushered to one side. Marjorie watched in dismay as the officials continued to deal with those behind him in the queue. What she didn't know was that the group of passengers behind him were on a mission for the Jewish relief organisation, JDC[1], who had been sent to oversee the aid given to thousands of Jewish displaced persons during the war. Gustave may well have been enlightened to this, so the attention they were receiving would have gained his respect. Though he was not a Jew, he had paid a heavy price for his anti-Nazi stance – a point which he was now having to prove to the Czech officials at the desk.

Marjorie turned to the young man behind her who was not one of the group. He seemed friendly.

'If you knew how I have worked to get these papers in order, and now this! It's as if we were not meant to be taking this journey. I have so dreaded it. Would you mind very much looking after the little one just for a few moments while I check what is holding things up?'

Handing the baby to the young man, she hurried towards the desk. Gustave came to meet her. 'Darling, don't worry. They're just being ultra-vigilant. You go ahead and get on the plane, get Baby settled. I won't be far behind.'

Marjorie was torn. How could she be certain they'd let him on the plane? Gustave caught the eye of the young man holding the baby.

Thank you for your help. May I introduce myself? I am Gustave Lange; this is my wife Marjorie and our little daughter. May I ask you to look after them both until I catch up? This is just a formality. I am told this is an inaugural flight arranged between the French and Czech Airlines; they are being ultra-vigilant due to my German surname.'

The young man, Jean, agreed readily. He was intrigued by the lady's perfect French, spoken with a distinctly

---

[1] Joint Distribution Committee (see p.263 and p.280)

English accent. Somewhat reassured, Marjorie allowed herself to be ushered away from her husband.

As they walked towards the plane, it looked tiny. She knew that the Junkers Ju-52 had been in military use throughout the war. Gustave had explained that the Czech airline had refurbished it for passenger use; this flight from Paris to Prague was its debut flight, carrying just eleven passengers and four crew.

Marjorie wasn't happy to be boarding without Gustave but knew it would be best to get the baby settled. Busying herself with her daughter, she tried to keep calm. If there were any real doubt about Gustave, the authorities would have held all three of them back, surely? She accepted gratefully Jean's offer to help with her hand baggage.

As he led her up the steps, Jean was hoping to get a seat as close to the front as possible. There, he thought, the prospects would be good for him to hear the instructions from air traffic control. As they boarded the aircraft, Jean was pleased that the flight crew waved them to the front.

Marjorie sank into the seat immediately behind the flight engineer and Jean sat down next to her. As half a dozen other passengers quickly filled the spaces around them, she twisted around trying to see if Gustave had finally been allowed to board. After everything they had overcome together, it would be too cruel if they were to be separated again so arbitrarily.

The challenges they had faced during the war had tested them both beyond all previous limits; they and everyone they knew had endured terrible hardship and loss. Marjorie was painfully aware how lucky they were now to be together. Having beaten such improbable odds to come through the misery of war, it seemed almost impossible to trust that nothing else could come between them. She prayed that their good fortune would not run out now.

To her great relief, Gustave appeared at the back just before the engines started up. He waved reassuringly as he was shown to one of the few remaining seats near the rear exit. Heart thudding, Marjorie closed her eyes in relief. Thank heavens for that – at least he'd made it onto the flight. It wasn't the end of the world if they weren't sitting together.

The baby slept soundly on her lap. Marjorie just wanted to get the whole thing over with. Now with a moment to reflect she stopped worrying about the journey and concerned herself more with the business which had to be done after their arrival in Prague. The sooner it could be done, the sooner they could get back to France. Then real decisions could be made about their future, to bring the family together again, finally, with James back home where he belonged.

They had been the recipients of yet more luck with their old friends. Marjorie's thoughts turned to Yvonne Bert-Datheil and her professor husband, who had arranged to put the family up overnight on their arrival. And Zantovski, their dear friend, had promised to be there to meet them. Settling back in her seat, Marjorie felt slightly calmer. Perhaps now she could relax.

The plane had taken off from Paris at 12.30 and was scheduled to make an intermediate stop at Strasbourg before arriving in Prague. Take-off had been smooth but Jean soon became aware that they were heading into bad weather. He had heard a few warnings whilst they were still on the ground, but Jean could tell that the captain was most concerned that this was a historic flight.

The plane was also carrying important French films for the very first Karlovy Vary (Karlsbad) Film Festival[2]; symbolic in terms of Franco/Czech relations. A Czech RAF pilot during the war who knew the route by heart, the captain was keen to get back to his family in Prague as soon as possible. He had decided the flight should proceed as planned, although Jean himself was beginning to doubt the wisdom of this decision.

Mid-flight, air traffic control suggested that they should not continue beyond Strasbourg to avoid the heavy snowfall threatening the airport in Prague. The captain acknowledged the suggestion but chose to go on.

Jean kept his growing discomfort to himself, not wishing to alarm the English lady who had been so anxious earlier. But his own training made him uneasy. Whyever would the pilot seemingly disregard the safety of his passengers and crew?

The descent was uneventful until they came through the clouds. Although night time, they could see snow driving hard against the windows. The poor visibility made it unsafe for the plane to land.

The captain's voice was perfectly calm. He assured the passengers they would be landing shortly, but he would circle the runway until they received instructions from air traffic control. By now Jean felt very anxious. He knew about planes. The wireless was very active and he felt increasingly on edge.

Marjorie had been half asleep when she heard the call, 'Fasten safety belts'. Still unconcerned, she wondered whether the Datheils would attempt to brave this dreadful weather in their car.

---

[2] Prominent guest: Rita Hayworth (see p.280)

The tiny plane circled several times in the snowstorm. Marjorie and Gustave's little daughter had been toddling up and down the aisle of the plane between her parents, but now Marjorie gathered her up onto her lap. Suddenly she was acutely aware of the soft spatter of snow against the window and the change in engine noise every time they gained height and then circled downwards again and again. Her stomach lurched and she swallowed fearfully. Every little noise seemed amplified.

Marjorie strained to hear what the flight crew appeared to be saying to one another. They were clearly making an effort to speak quietly – did they know something the passengers did not? To her horror she heard that visibility was so poor that the second pilot had been obliged to open the window, but still they could see nothing. In addition, fog was now compounding the problem. Marjorie listened in dread as passengers behind her peered out of the windows and wondered aloud to each other how the pilots could possibly see where they were going.

The plane lurched once more and there was a sudden loss of height. A momentary silence fell over the cabin, increasing her awareness of the engine noise. This was quickly broken by concerned murmurs; people in the seats behind her were openly discussing what could be happening. The baby began to cry, quickly becoming inconsolable. Aware of increasing panic, Marjorie tried desperately to pacify her, murmuring over and over that it was only an air pocket. Calming the child helped to some extent to keep her own fears in perspective. Turning her head, she strained to catch Gustave's eye but his seat was out of her sight. The baby's cries pierced another uneasy silence and she held her daughter more firmly on her lap, trying to counteract the queasy lurching of the plane.

They continued to gain height and then spiral downwards. Twisting around in her seat, Marjorie bent to kiss her daughter's head and tried once more to see Gustave. The only faces in view belonged to the other passengers, white and terrified. Some were even praying aloud. She glanced towards the windows, raking the panes for a clue but all were white, unseeing eyes. The swirling snow and fog killed any hope of working out their proximity to the ground.

Marjorie fought down a powerful instinct to leave her seat and run down the aisle with the baby to be with her husband. She dared not unfasten her belt. Gripped by fear, she closed her eyes as the plane spiralled downwards once more and the engines screamed.

CHAPTER TWO

FROM DRUDGERY TO DANCE

The bravery and determination that would stand Marjorie in such good stead throughout the Second World War had been forged during an often difficult childhood. She and her two older sisters were the eldest of twelve children; from an early age they were expected to assume many childcare duties as well as household chores. There never seemed enough of anything to go around. All three left home as early as it was prudent to do so, nursing a grim determination to escape the hardships they had endured during their early years.

Marjorie did well at school and at the age of fifteen opted to train as a nurse. She found a post as a children's help and nurse, living in with a well-off family, the Hendersons, in Southampton – an escape route that she knew would secure her parents' approval.

However, she found little fulfilment in that role. Life for everyone else in the Henderson household revolved around the theatre. The Hendersons were self-styled impresarios. They had met on the stage and built their entire married lives around it. It appeared to Marjorie that their children certainly took second place.

Witnessing for the first time a world devoid of domestic chores and childcare, Marjorie's imagination was captured by the excitement and colour. Talk was always of the next production, the grand tour, rehearsals, casting and whether or not the last leading lady would be up to the next job. A constant stream of visitors flounced in and out of the house, and voices raised by many a temperamental prima donna afforded Marjorie much entertainment. The glamour and vibrancy of these visitors were infectious; she longed to be one of them.

Growing up, Marjorie had heard the steamers sailing across Southampton Water to distant shores and often watched them on the tide of her imagination. She was becoming more and more aware of the possibilities life away from her childhood home might hold.

Marjorie at 16 years of age

Marjorie was greatly taken by the pictures of leading ladies in the programmes of West End productions. She had her own portrait photographed twice: once in

Cardiff, visiting the Parisienne in Duke Street aged sixteen during a visit to her sister Flora; the other in a Putney studio, her bare shoulders trimmed with organza. Now, her drive was directed towards a much more exciting life.

George Henderson rather liked Marjorie's walk. In fact, there was something about that walk he'd spotted quite early on. He mentioned it more than once to his wife Alice, who was already wrestling with her own conscience over what she now perceived was the mismatch between Marjorie and the role for which she'd been employed.

This posed a problem; they were very fond of Marjorie and had noted approvingly that her lack of enjoyment in her work had not dimmed her efforts to do the job well, or indeed her popularity with the children. The Hendersons privately agreed that the qualities they found so attractive in her were well suited for the stage. She was completely untrained, of course, but this could be an advantage; they could mould her to the many roles which they found difficult to cast.

In any case, they decided, Marjorie must be offered a start in various backstage jobs before she was to have any chance as a performer; one needed a thorough grounding in every aspect of the business. Nothing was said until they had made alternative arrangements for the children. Once this was dealt with, Marjorie was ecstatic to be given such an opportunity, especially with the Paris tour looming.

She started in the theatre by helping out behind the scenes, with the props or sometimes in makeup but dreamed of her own starring role in Paris. Her days, though full and tiring, were tinged with the glamour of performance and her confidence was growing. Marjorie longed for her own moment in the spotlight. The distance from her family enabled a wider view of the world; she was thankful for the Hendersons' patronage.

Her parents would certainly not understand her longing for the stage.

There was never any show business in Marjorie's family. Marjorie's mother, Lily Ethel, was a lady in all but name; her daughter was under no illusions as to the expected trajectory of her own life.

Lily had been born in East Cowes on the Isle of Wight, her family tree reaching back to the Roberton family, prominent for more than a century for its ownership of the ferry rights from East to West Cowes over that part of the river Medina called The Point. Through the Robertons, Lily was related to Uffa Fox, whose inventions made a huge contribution to the war effort, though he was best known for his association both as a friend and master yachtsman to Prince Philip.

Marjorie knew that her mother's family had been the ones to invent a system to winch a barge back and forth by ropes to convey carts, carriages and horses across the river. In 1859, twenty years before Lily's birth, they had sold the ferry rights to a company formed for the construction of the very first steam-driven chain floating bridge. The floating bridge was an important and impressive part of life on the coast even now.

Marjorie's father was also from a well-respected, though perhaps less illustrious, seafaring family. A handsome lad and the source of great pride to his mother, Will Derham had a good brain and a sharp wit. He loved to tell a good joke and was known among his friends and family to be a straight talker. Though he was often blunt, Marjorie admired her father greatly. She appreciated straightforwardness in a person –people always knew where they stood with him.

Will Derham in his early twenties

Will was proud of his trade. He had served his apprenticeship as a boilermaker at White's Shipyard in Cowes. Will and Lily had plenty in common; both were the children of Master Mariners living with widowed mothers when they fell in love aged 21.

They were married in East Cowes parish church on 30th June 1901 and set up home in Cowes, famous for its annual regatta as well as Osborne House, designed by Prince Albert as a family retreat and so loved by Queen Victoria that it became her favourite refuge after his death. One of very few tall, three storey houses in Osborne Road, Rose Cottage belied its name and provided a substantial family home for the Derhams, becoming the birthplace of ten of their twelve children.

While close to Osborne House in distance, Osborne Road was far removed from it in every other respect. The house belonged to Will's grandparents, backing on to the nursery which had provided their livelihood until retirement. When the grandparents reached old age, the family made the house available to Will and Lily so that they could keep an eye on the old folk. It was always a full house; as the grandparents died, their number was far outweighed by a new generation of babies.

Olive, Flora and Dorothy were born in each successive year after their parents' marriage, but Dorothy died one winter at the age of ten months after a very short illness. The blow was devastating. Marjorie was born two years later in 1906 to a still mourning mother. Mona followed in 1908, Jack in 1909, Beryl in 1911 and Bill in 1912. Lily was glad that for two and a half years there followed a 'nice long rest from child bearing' before Eileen was born in 1914. She died within six weeks.

In September of that year, World War One was declared. By then Marjorie was approaching eight years old. Just before her ninth birthday, Maurice was born and died. It had been a terrible year.

When it came, the Great War dictated significant changes in their lives. Working ceaselessly to look after their large family while still grieving for her lost babies, Lily feared that Will would have to enlist with most of his compatriots to fight. She was greatly relieved when instead he was offered the chance to move to the dockyard in Southampton.

Will's trade was an important facet to the ship building industry; in wartime as much labour as possible was needed, so his skills were at a premium.

Southampton Docks was the home of all the great liners, he told Lily; firms like De Havilland would be kept busy meeting the demands of the war at sea. They must move to the mainland.

In thirteen years at Rose Cottage, Lily had borne and nursed ten babies, but only seven children moved in with them towards the end of 1915 to the terraced house with a bay window in Southampton. While smaller than Rose Cottage, 23 Union Street was only a short walk from the docks, near the farm school and open land around Mount Pleasant.

Times may have been very hard throughout the Great War, but life became still more difficult afterwards when the demands from the shipyard dried up. The strain took its toll, especially on the three eldest children who often had to look after the babies and support their mother in every possible way. This drew the girls closer together and a special bond developed between Marjorie and Bill. Marjorie was nine years old and her brother just three when they moved – she became like a little mother to him.

In their new school in Southampton, Marjorie's sister Mona was told by her teacher that she was a good pupil, but it was her sister Marjorie who would 'make her mark'. Flora and Jack did show signs of academic brilliance; both won scholarships to private schools[3], but their father rejected these on the basis that all his children must be treated on equal terms.

Will was now away from home for long periods, settling wherever he could find enough work to sustain

---

[3] Leslie Jack Derham was posthumously awarded a gold medal by the Royal Society for his outstanding contribution to Science. The Mullard Medal was presented to his widow, Gwen at the Dorchester Hotel, London on 30th November 1970

the family. Despite his efforts, there came a time when their basic needs simply were not met. The youngest girl, Beryl, was sent away to Will's sister and her husband who were teachers. A revered and respected profession, teaching was also secure: not subject to the fluctuations of the marketplace, nor the vagaries of war.

These early experiences had a profound effect on the formation of all the children's characters and the speed with which they fled the nest. The Derham girls were all driven by a strong sense of purpose. The boys, on the other hand, had a rather a casual air about them. Down to earth like Will and with a string of older sisters to nurture them in childhood, they grew up bright, confident and well equipped to secure good jobs. Much to their mother's delight, years later all were engaged in vital industries, thus rendering them indispensable to their employers and ruling out conscription to the armed forces.

The older girls had an additional common denominator – the drive for a better life. Olive resolved to 'marry a gentleman,' and this she did. An officer in the Guards, he was many years her senior and willing to indulge her taste for fine furniture and lovely pieces of porcelain. Olive's daughters were raised to be young ladies and educated at a private school for girls.

Mona's need to control her own destiny and get value for money stayed with her for life. She found great delight in bargains too good to resist at Mrs Nunn's junk shop, which transformed into objéts d'art once they adorned her rather grand homes. At eighteen, she too married a much older man, though that union was short-lived. Mona was green-fingered like her grandparents and ran a market garden with her second husband, a nurseryman and beekeeper. This paid its way until somehow the bees got rather more attention than the books and all was nearly lost. They did recover, but Mona was to spend widowhood managing her money very carefully, anxious to ensure she would never be placed in such a position again.

For seventeen-year-old Marjorie, the prospect of living within the narrow parameters of parental approval had been far from appealing. And now, more than a year later, she saw the water, that ever-present backdrop to her childhood, less as a barrier to the rest of the world and more as a passage to take her wherever she wanted to go. Entranced by the notion of a glamorous world beyond her own, Marjorie dreamed endlessly of Paris, home of the Ballet Russes and epicentre of chic. She watched the performers from her backstage duties with an increasing determination to achieve her own role in the spotlight before long. When the Hendersons finally suggested taking her to Paris, she could hardly believe it. The opportunity had finally arisen to escape drudgery, duty and family ties and she grabbed it with both hands. Packing her belongings for the trip, Marjorie was elated. She would make the most of every moment.

CHAPTER THREE

A NEW LIFE IN PARIS

Paris in the summer of 1925 was paradise to Marjorie. She had travelled with the small dance company via packet board across the water from England and by rail to the Gare St Lazare. Paris was breathtakingly beautiful with its fine buildings and wide boulevards; with the steps, cobbled streets and markets of Montmartre rising behind them and the many little restaurants and cabarets. There was little motor traffic; horse drawn fiacres still plied their trade and the sound of motor horns mingled with the clatter of clopping hooves, the rattle of trams and street traders' cries. Theatres and art galleries were thriving and the underground Metro was the first in Europe. The silver river wound its way past the old centre around Notre Dame, past the Louvre and continued westwards, where elegant new suburbs were developing close to the mysteriously beautiful Bois de Bologne.

This was a far cry from her traditional English childhood. Instead of smoking chimney stacks, cloth caps and relentless poverty, she saw decorative ironwork on elegant buildings, and smart suited, trilbyed men going purposefully about their business. Marjorie imagined herself sitting on delicate scrolled chairs outside pavement cafes. She gazed at the high heeled ladies, always immaculately dressed in the latest fashions, and yearned to be one of them. Of course, the Hendersons were chaperones for the benefit of gaining her father's consent, but their young charge was relieved that they were free thinkers like herself. She felt sure they would prove no impediment to her new life.

Although young and naïve, Marjorie did possess self-confidence and poise. Her energy and excitement meant that when she walked into a room the place lit up. Although not a natural beauty, she was strikingly attractive. Brunette hair with auburn lights and deep blue eyes set off a *retroussé* nose much admired by the French. About five feet six inches tall, Marjorie's long legs and shapely shoulders, along with a generous bosom, gave her a sadly unfashionable hourglass silhouette entirely unsuited to the boyish flapper fashions of the time. Busts were decidedly out; Marjorie, like many other young women, went to extraordinary lengths to disguise her curves, binding her chest tightly to try to flatten it.

The little company numbered no more than a dozen including the Hendersons, who did everything from producing, directing and performing to curating the tours and coordinating travel arrangements. A little troupe of eight or nine players came and went, and Marjorie was fascinated to see how their diverse mix of talent created the shows. A more permanent additional fixture was Jerry the stage hand. Marjorie had already witnessed his magical transformations of the most dismally utilitarian backdrop into a kaleidoscope of scenes. It was easy to imagine the audience feeling as though they'd been transported into another world.

Their repertoire included a number of musical adaptations, the occasional farce and their most popular production: a topical revue. Most of the *ensemble* were able to play at least one instrument – here, to her chagrin, Marjorie simply could not compete. Nevertheless, she gained her grounding, first as a general assistant and then in the props department; it was great fun sourcing whichever bits and pieces were needed to bring the production to life. After a short-lived stint at painting scenery, Marjorie's creative eye was transferred to the dressing room, where she learned to apply just the right amount of makeup to turn ordinary people into stars.

From the incessant rehearsals she got to know every line of dialogue, every note of music, but it was many months before Marjorie had the chance to take part in an actual performance.

Nita was older and had been with the company for nearly two years. A beautiful dancer and full of fun, she was tall with long dark hair and brown eyes. Nita was a responsible girl, the Hendersons agreed, and an ideal companion for Marjorie. They charged her with keeping a watchful eye on their young protégée, arranging that the girls should share a little *pension* close to Montmartre and the old theatre which was to be their place of work for a season.

Marjorie and Nita soon became the best of friends. On days off they explored the city, taking tram rides into the Latin Quarter and getting to know some of the cafes frequented by groups of young artists and intellectuals. They often took long walks along the Champs Elysées, the banks of the Seine or in the Bois de Bologne, soaking up the atmosphere of their new surroundings. Marjorie revelled in her glamorous new life.

Once they were settled, Nita encouraged her friend to take dancing lessons and join in with daily rehearsals. Much of the Paris show was a collection of offerings from the young Noel Coward, accompanied by dance and sometimes risqué little soliloquies.

First used as an extra, Marjorie was soon playing more than one part, although still largely minor roles. Alex, one of the male dancers, was a real encouragement to her. He loved being with the girls, even presenting Marjorie with an inscribed, framed picture of himself, which first of all hung in their dressing room but accompanied her well into her future life. Before long the dancing lessons enabled her to become part of the chorus line, which she adored. The most exciting and novel experience for her was the audience. Months of rehearsals and backstage work had not prepared her for the euphoria of standing ovations.

This dreamlike existence was enhanced by the profusion of flowers which would appear in the dressing room she shared with Nita and Gloria. Sometimes marked *pour la fille dans la robe rouge* or just *pour Marjorie*, the excitement of these offerings was tempered by Nita's obdurate protection, standing guard at the stage door against over-zealous admirers. Although she trusted her friend's judgement, Marjorie found the restraint very frustrating on occasion.

She began to get to know the other two girls. Nita was the funny one, always clowning around, but Marjorie found Gloria difficult to like at first. She held herself aloof from the others, having once or twice been given a supporting role to one of the touring artists who would receive top billing for special guest performances at intervals throughout the season. A leggy blonde with a particularly good voice, Gloria was well aware of her advantages. One evening, she became quite cruel to Marjorie for receiving more attention at the stage door than she herself did. Marjorie's self-confidence tended to abandon her whenever she was faced with hostility, relying on Nita to come to her rescue. Marjorie came to depend quite heavily on her older roommate.

As weeks became months the theatre drew larger and larger audiences. *La compagnie* was gaining wonderful reviews, but the contract which the Hendersons had so carefully drawn up with the Montmartre venue was coming to an end. Insecurity was mounting, engendering the inevitable disquiet among the cast.

One day during rehearsals, Alice Henderson swept into the theatre excitedly waving papers at George. After a fleeting glimpse and a whoop of delight, he jumped on stage and announced that they'd been invited to take the show on a grand tour of the provinces. The joy with which this news was received became ecstatic when he confirmed that all who wished to stay on would receive a considerable pay rise.

When the final curtain came down on the Montmartre theatre, the entire company held a party backstage and invited some of the regular devotees. Marjorie had never experienced anything quite like it: wine flowed, smiles and chatter gave way to fun and games, then someone suggested going on to *Gentils'*, a little restaurant in the shadow of the Cathedral.

The Gentils were a young couple who had met while training in the kitchen of one of the high class hotels just off the Champs Elysées. They had been fortunate to obtain some backing from their respective families to open their restaurant. *Gentils'* had only been open a few weeks with modest take up when *la petite compagnie Anglaise* burst into their lives. On this occasion, *petite* was far from the case. Complete with guests, the entire company descended on their hosts amid great excitement. Somehow the Gentils managed to accommodate them all and presented them with a meal fitting for an end of season celebration.

That evening transformed this young couple's small venture; from then on, for many years to come *Gentils'* came to life every night when much of Parisian society was getting ready for bed. It became the place to go after the final curtain call and a general meeting point for actors, artists, musicians and various hangers-on.

During the short break before the show went on the road, Marjorie and Nita contemplated their improved finances, planning how they would transform themselves into *dames élégantes*. Paris was already the centre of haute couture; Marjorie knew exactly how she would spend her money. Every night, as the curtain came down and the lights went up, she had watched with admiration and envy the style – *le chic* – which set certain ladies in the audience apart from the rest. Those in the *fauteils d'orchestre*, where it was usual for full evening dress to be worn, were often absolutely stunning. Marjorie longed to be able to emulate them.

The Twenties had ushered in a complete revolution in fashion, the end of the Great War contributing to a desire to be free from constraint. Gone were sweeping full length skirts flowing from nipped waistlines, to be replaced with provocatively short hemlines attached to straight, drop-waisted bodices. Legs were now on display and silk stockings were all the rage. Long strings of beads adorned the new styles, along with headbands from which peacock feathers stood proud. High heeled, pointed shoes gave ankles a new and exciting limelight. By 1924 Coco Chanel had made her mark by contributing some ground-breaking costume designs for Diaghilev's *Le Train Bleu* and the following year (only months before Marjorie) Josephine Baker arrived in Paris to stun audiences when she performed the *Danse Sauvage* with dance partner Joe Alex, topless, wearing only a feather skirt. She wore her famous banana hip girdle a year later at the Folies-Bergere.

Nothing quite so exotic was sought by Marjorie, whose window shopping expeditions with Nita now replaced their earlier, more general explorations. The girls imagined themselves soon to be draped in the latest finery. Marjorie wondered what her sisters would think of her good fortune and whether to write and tell them of her news. Concerned that her luck may run out, she decided to wait until the tour was under way and the Hendersons' payday promises could be realized.

Travelling to Nantes, Rennes and Rouen, every venue drew bigger audiences than the one before. Marjorie could hardly believe how well known the show had become; by the time they reached Caen they were performing before full houses night after night. In time, one or two of the company were invited as special guests for cameo performances in cabaret. These appearances at some of the smartest hotels and casinos, both in town and some of the holiday resorts like Deauville and Trouville on the Normandy *Cote Nacre* [Mother of Pearl Coast], widened their horizons enormously.

They were now far more engaged with audiences: after the show, they were the ones entertained and treated to drinks, making new friends and dancing into the early hours.

Despite the constant round of invitations to return to previous venues, Paris once more became their focus. Over time this little group of individuals became a highly polished professional team, creating subtle improvisations 'on the hoof' to accommodate different audiences and locations. The show was gradually transformed from a string of musical sketches punctuated with a variety of dance routines, into a beautifully choreographed performance which flowed from start to finish, enchanting audiences which demanded encore after encore. Early difficulties with language were now being mastered to such a degree that they all had to work hard at keeping their English accents, which were a major part of their attraction.

There was still no shortage of admirers. Marjorie had learned from Nita the art of enjoying the advances of men drawn to the mystique and glamour of the performance, without allowing them too close, thus increasing the attraction several-fold. Keeping them all at arm's length, she could have many boyfriends and was never short of an escort after a show or on her evenings off. This strategy continued to pay off for quite some time without the encumbrance of emotional attachment. Marjorie knew that if she were to fall in love herself, this convenient social whirl might unravel very quickly. For now, though, there seemed no danger of that.

One evening, the three girls and Alex had been engaged to perform at the Casino at St. Aubin. Marjorie immediately noticed the handsome man at the piano. He had dark hair, a tanned complexion and an engaging smile: so engaging that she found it difficult to avoid his glance, which seemed to be in her direction whenever she turned his way. She wondered if he were the resident pianist. He certainly knew how to play and was able to pick up their musical piece as though he played it every night.

Their act was greeted with hearty applause from those still enjoying their coffee and *digestifs* at the end of a meal. After the final encore, Marjorie and the others took their bows, as did the young musician. Before they could retreat to their dressing rooms he was there, excusing himself in fluent English although the accent was not the familiar French one. Eyes fixed on Marjorie, he complimented them all on their performance.

'Please give me the honour of joining me at my table.'

They accepted his invitation, which drew excited commentary all the way back to the dressing room. This well-dressed young man was not only good looking but appeared to be far more of a gentleman than their usual crowd of followers. His fixation on Marjorie had not escaped the others' notice and she was the subject of much teasing which continued, somewhat suppressed, even after they joined his table. Thankfully he was not alone, so their banter was soon part of the general conversation and Marjorie tried to regain her composure. It was some time before the chatter abated sufficiently for him to make the introductions. But eventually, and apologising for this delay, he said,

'May I introduce you to my friends Jean and Pierre, and my name is Gustave...'

Offering Marjorie the seat next to him, he seemed very keen to talk. It was not long before she discovered that he was Czech, had worked in London, and was now working in Paris. Marjorie was impressed that his English and his French were both very nearly perfect: this was certainly an educated man.

She didn't yet know that Gustave had inherited his large hazel eyes and the smile which dimpled his cheeks from his mother. These attributes, coupled with a sporty physique thanks to his love of swimming and tennis, did nothing to dim his attractiveness. His new acquaintances were charmed by his confident and engaging manner, but Marjorie felt oddly discomfited. This popular and accomplished young man with his worldly charm came as a shock after so many more predictable admirers. She was undeniably attracted to him, but couldn't help but wonder whether his apparent interest would wane if he got to know her. He seemed infinitely more exotic than anyone she'd ever met back in Southampton. Her habitual confidence wavered as she tried to appear relaxed in his company, sure that he would notice her nerves.

CHAPTER FOUR

ROMANCE ARRIVES WITH GUSTAVE

According to Gustave, at that time French men had a simple way of describing their taste in women by dividing them into two categories: apples and willows. Apples having a series of round, curvy shapes like Marilyn Monroe. Willows being tall, lean and angular, best suited to the catwalk. Marjorie was undoubtedly an apple.

Gustave was an apple-loving man. He could not explain the glow he felt when he thought of her. Nita had been her usual protective self at the end of their evening together at the Casino; all the girls had enjoyed themselves, but no addresses were given and no promises exchanged. Nita was probably the more beautiful, but it was Marjorie who occupied his mind to the exclusion of all else. Somewhat overtaken by these feelings, he was irritated with himself for being so out of control. Gustave considered himself a romantic and had always prided himself on his charm, but this was the first time he had felt so completely overwhelmed. Trying and failing not to think about this girl, he eventually decided he would have to go to the theatre to find her.

There was something about an English Rose. The girls in the show were all lovely, with porcelain complexions and those charming accents. The performance held him spellbound, but eventually the curtain came down. Carefully dressed in a crisp dark suit and sparkling white shirt, he finally presented himself at the stage door with flowers and chocolates for Marjorie.

Having gone home the night before firmly resolved to keep him at a distance, now she was dazzled. The *frisson* which passed between them was so intense; she felt unnerved. Attempting nonchalance, she thanked him graciously for the gifts but her usual confidence and wit deserted her and she struggled to find enough words for polite conversation.

'What on earth is happening to me?' she wondered silently as he repeatedly came to her rescue.

Before long, Gustave escorted Marjorie to a restaurant near the seafront. A glass or two of wine soon fortified her, and by the end of the meal she was relieved that they seemed to be chatting like old friends.

After that first encounter, they continued to enjoy each other's company for some time. Marjorie, fearful that revealing her true feelings may spoil the friendship, continued rather feebly to try to keep Gustave at arm's length. In April 1927 *la petite compagnie Anglaise* was commissioned for a two-month tour of Europe. Marjorie wondered if this timely intervention would afford them both space to test their true feelings. They would be apart for the whole of May and June.

For now, though, they were together. The couple had often visited Montmorency, a short walk from the small lakeside town of Enghien with its casino. Strolling carefree through the picturesque streets of the old town, they followed the ancient mossy walls which wound their way past peaceful townhouses. This April, however, their usual delight in the setting was tempered by the looming separation.

The fruit trees formed clouds of white pear blossom humming with bees. The beauty of their surroundings and the charged atmosphere heightened emotions; both now knew they were in love. As they kissed and held each other, he begged her to remember him while she was away. When Gustave confessed his love she listened happily but did not commit herself, yet, to a reply. Overwhelmed by her own feelings, Marjorie needed time to think.

Gustave had arrived in Paris from London three years earlier and had been working for Arnold Grief at Number Seven, Rue Bergere for all of that time.

Nearly four weeks after Marjorie's departure he received an unexpected visit from his younger brother, Karli. It was a welcome surprise; he needed cheering up. He still had not heard from her. During the evening he was glad to be able to unburden himself.

Ironically, the purpose of Karli's visit seemed to add weight to Gustave's new situation: it presented him with both a problem and a solution in one.

'Look, Gustl,' said Karli, 'a vacancy has arisen at home with Ginzkey, and old Glazer really wants you to have the job'.

Gustave was amazed that he should be the subject of such interest from the Maffersdorf firm after all these years. Karli had established himself very well there; the Lange family was well respected. However, Glazer knew that Gustl's language skills were just what they needed in the new post of International Representative. No other likely candidate would have his experience in London and Paris.

'Karli,' he replied, 'Would *you* even think of leaving all this behind? I'm sorry, I'm having too good a time. I can't go back to Maffersdorf, it would just be a step backwards. Tell Josef I'm really grateful that he thought of me, but it's out of the question.' He paused. 'I doubt they could afford me anyway.'

Gustave could see that his brother was disappointed but he didn't pursue it. There was no contest. They enjoyed the rest of the evening together and laughed about Karli's latest exploits. He too was a ladies' man, never without several to entertain him, but love had so far eluded him. They ended the evening dancing the Charleston at a smart casino and, for the moment at least, Gustave's heartache was forgotten.

It returned, with a headache to boot, when he awoke the next morning. He bade farewell to Karli, who left with the words, 'Are you still sure…?'

Gustave nodded his reply. Paris was now in his blood – the prospect of going back home after five years away did little to excite him. In any case, he was missing his lovely woman after only a few weeks. How could he think of leaving her forever?

The prospect of marriage at this stage, however, had barely crossed his mind but Maffersdorf was so far removed from the life Marjorie was used to. There seemed no point in giving it a second thought.

Gustave was very unsettled. Since their parting he could think of nothing else. Then to his delight he received a short letter from her in which she said she loved him. His burden lifted instantly. In his reply to 'My dearest own little woman', dated Paris, 19th May '27, he wrote:

I have your dear letter and am so happy to hear you love me. The first nice letter you wrote me since you have gone, only it was too short…

If only these four weeks were already over and I could see you entering this room and take you *enfin* in my arms. I am so unhappy without you, Beloved, and never knew I would miss you so much. I feel no joy nor pleasure. I am quite sure my heart has gone with you, or I should feel at least something, but I am just living and my inside is <u>dead</u>. So please Dearest, do come back as soon as you can and make your Gustl happy again. I wonder so much if you will have changed…

Correspondence between them became fast and furious. In reply to her letter from Spain he closes with these words:

Dearest, I am so happy to hear that you still say your prayers. I think it was too beautiful when I could hold your dear hands in mine. Do you often think of those moments? I am missing you now so <u>much</u>. My only wish will ever be that our prayers are joined in heaven, like our hearts and souls on earth.
With all my thoughts and love
Your Gustave
Hope to hear from you tomorrow!

A business trip to Luc sur Mer helped a little to take Gustave's mind off things. He made himself very popular with his fellow guests and the hotel patron, who promised him a commission to play the piano. However, none of the distractions he gave himself provided more than just a brief respite from his heartache such that when two more letters arrived his only thought was to write her this lengthy reply:

Luc sur mer, Tuesday
My dearest own little woman

Just a few lines as I am going this afternoon to Caen and shall not come back before tonight. I was so happy this morning when I found your two letters on the breakfast plate. Dearest, now I wish so much that you are having a nice time. Soonly, I shall come back to you and hold you in my arms at night. I too am sure that I love you and always pray to God that my love will be sufficient to make you happy for all your life.

Last Sunday we went in a lovely car to St Aubin to the new Casino. It is a nice little place and I danced nearly every dance until I was wet to the skin. I was presented to the maire who offered a champagne banquet that lasted until late in the morning. Yesterday, I have taken my first bath in the sea with those two English boys. The poor kids felt so lonely. They told me they had been taken out by a French doctor to a place with girls and as they didn't kiss the girls he was no longer interested in them. I had to laugh. I sent them to Dinard and then to Paris...In the morning we play tennis and after lunch we have nice walks. Since I am here I dream all the night through and often so awfully that I wake up early in the morning. I can feel that there is something missing beside me and then I have to think so much of you while smoking a cigarette.

I wished you had heard already from Olive. What do you think about it? And how is Nita? You say nothing about her. I am sending her a card by same post. Now I am going to play 'The Millions d'Arlekin' for you. I thought about that something that you have had done for me and suppose it is your hair. I hope I will find it nice too. Please give my kindest regards to Gloria, Jerry, Mr and Mrs Henderson as well as to your car man, also my love to Nita.

God bless you and keep you good
Your own loving man, Gustave

Gustave's tales of Marjorie's tour elicited suggestions from his boss that he should have enlisted her services as a buyer. When Marjorie wrote from Germany she indignantly recounted a confrontation she'd had with a woman who was teaching her the wrong kind of German. He was horrified that the words she was being taught were 'bad' words, writing on the same notepaper from Luc Sur Mer:

> Sunday morning
> Mein lieber Schatz
> So glad I received a letter this morning saying you and Nita are well. You are, no doubt, practicing for a German guide. I only wonder how much you did understand of that bad German woman's talk and how much you supposed to do. Perhaps Mr Greif discovered already your abilities and that's why he thinks to engage you as a buyer.
> Dearest, in my last night's letter you will find half of the rose I slept with last night. It will tell you how happy it has been under my kisses...I just have been in the water and am still trembling as you can see. The water is rather warm but there is no sunshine this morning to get dry on the sands. Our terrace is full of people – for it is Sunday. The patron of our hotel as well as of those near to us have promised me already, a commission for playing the piano.
> Last week we went by car all along the coast to Cabourg, Deauville and Trouville. It was a most beautiful ride. Also, I have been invited to stay here until the end of August but how could I live without my Marjorie and her kisses? Sweetheart, why can we not be rich like all these people – on the other hand I would for nothing in the world give them our happiness and you not either, nicht wahr, mein Leibling. It must be meant by God that these people are more or less unhappy.
> Bye Bye, dearest own, and God Bless you. Don't break too many men's hearts. I love you!!!

Your own man Gustave

When Marjorie returned, Gustave was back in Paris and their longed-for reunion was all it promised to be. They went back to Montmorency often, at other times taking long walks into the Bois de Boulogne. Gustave was sure now that this was the woman he wanted to marry, but could see no practical means of gaining the financial security to enable him, in all conscience, to propose.

Then out of the blue on 27th July came a letter from Josef Glazer in Maffersdorf:

Dear Mr Lange

In your previous correspondence with your brother Karli you sent me the message that you were not interested in the prospective post of travelling representative for the Firm I. Ginzkey which was then in view, because you still had to complete a certain part of your planned programme of gaining experience abroad.

Meanwhile this post has become free and a decision must soon be taken as to which of the mass of candidates who have presented themselves should be chosen. As I believe I can guess that you have not been correctly informed of the kind of position this is, I would like, purely as a goodwill gesture, to set clearly before you the fact that this is definitely a prestigious career position, combined with duties which are easy and pleasant to fulfil. The countries Denmark, Sweden, Norway, Finland, Switzerland and Germany are to be visited twice a year and the rest of the time (almost a third of the year is set aside for preparations and conferences in Maffersdorf) is strictly speaking a rest period. The salary is a very good one, besides a satisfactory basic salary there is also a percentage share in the turnover, which together amounts to a very respectable sum. The travelling allowances are not niggardly and certainly provide for a good lifestyle when travelling, allowing other income to be saved.

I am setting out this outline today, without prejudice, with the request that you telegraph me at once whether you wish to stand by your first decision or whether you would like now to be considered as a candidate for the post. Mr Alfred Mallmann will in fact be arriving in Paris within the next few days on his way back from New York, probably staying at the Hotel Mirabeau, and I will then let you know by telegram when you could present yourself to him. In order to avoid wasting any time, please would you also advise me of your Paris address.

I would ask you however, not to alter any present plans of any kind because of my letter today. In other words, if you are not interested in this matter, I should be content to receive a few lines on the subject but if you are to meet Mr Mallmann, I would do my utmost to support your application on his return.

With best wishes,
Yours
Josef H Glazer

This time Gustave gave it serious thought. Perhaps the position *would* give him the stature and security that marriage required. And perhaps he could persuade Ginzkey to have Paris as his base. He decided there was nothing to lose by meeting Mallmann, so he telegraphed his interest and address to Maffersdorf the same day.

The meeting was a success; Mr Mallmann took back with him a formal application and some good references. Within days Gustave was invited to Maffersdorf for an interview on 22nd August with the top man, Mr Willy Ginzkey. In the same letter, Glazer wrote,

> You will certainly be pleased with the conditions – you need not worry about them in the least. If you are

appointed, a rich field of activity will lie open before you from which you can aspire, with care and hard work, to great success...

It is important that you should be able to take up the position soon. I intend to give you the first 3-4 weeks in Maffersdorf to get to know the articles and the customers. Then the first journey through Southern Germany and Switzerland will begin followed, after a short break, by the tour of the northern lands. I am convinced you will enjoy the work.

It seemed like a foregone conclusion. Gustave, now nearing the point of no return, wondered how he would break the news to Marjorie. He didn't want to risk losing her but knew he'd be foolish to pass up this opportunity to advance his career. Anyway, he reassured himself, it was just an interview. He didn't have to commit himself yet.

Gradually Gustave found himself warming to the idea of seeing his parents again. Would they find him changed? For the better, he hoped. They would of course be delighted if he took the offer. He knew that they were proud of their boy; this prestigious position would be much discussed and exclaimed over, not just within the Lange family but the neighbouring households in their little village. He shuddered at the prospect of their response if he chose not to take the job.

To his relief, Marjorie was very supportive. She didn't want to stand in the way of such an opportunity and encouraged him to go. Secretly, Marjorie suspected that the offer would fall far short of Paris levels of remuneration; she drew comfort from her conviction that he would return in a couple of weeks. Since the last separation, the two had become tightly bound together in their love. The atmosphere the evening before

Gustave's departure was heavy with mixed emotions: a nervousness which neither could understand nor explain, mutual reassurance, repeated pronouncements of their love for each other, the whole culminating in irresistible passion.

The next day he set off alone on his journey with a heavy heart. If the trip was successful, he knew there would be little choice but to accept it. If separation was the only way for him to be in a position to marry, then it would be worth it. Although he hadn't voiced these thoughts to Marjorie, he felt the new job was probably the only way of achieving his greatest wish: to have her by his side forever.

CHAPTER FIVE

MAFFERSDORF, REICHENBERG

At the time of Gustave's birth in 1900, the Bohemian Sudetenland was part of the Austro-Hungarian empire under Emperor Franz Josef. Reichenberg was a well-established town of some standing – the United States had a Vice Consul there – with cloth factories and spinning mills. Grouped around the *Altstaedter Platz* [Old Town Square], a large cobbled square with a fountain, were the Rathaus, the old and the new Town Hall, the latter completed in 1893, and some interesting arcaded buildings. All were signs of progress, prosperity, civic pride and possibly an ancient charter as a borough.

By the twentieth century a substantial theatre had been built, the North Bohemian Industrial Museum had opened and there was a municipal picture gallery, a gondola pond, botanical garden, parks and a large reservoir. There was also a Business School and elegant cafés where burghers and intellectuals met, including the Café Reichshof which Gustave mentions in one of his letters. Banking had produced at least one wealthy and influential family, the Bischoffs.

The town boasted tradition, culture, educational opportunities and a thriving active community. It was a matter of great pride to Gustave in 1931 that the sound version of *Ben Hur* reached Reichenberg soon after its premiere in Paris.

An industrious drive to improve their lot in life was a particular feature of the three million Sudeten Germans in Czechoslovakia, reflected in the succession of occupations held by their ancestors. The eighteenth century home-based industry of making stockings is evident over three generations, alongside the weaving skills of the Porsches and Panitschkas. The Lange family had made the shift from farmer to gardener and from stocking worker to weaver. Ferdinand Porsche[4], founder of the famous Volkswagen car manufacturer, was born in the same village as Josef Lange and his early interest in electricity was served by regular visits to Ginzkey, the same firm which employed Karli and was now inviting Gustave to join its success.

The increasing importance of weaving was evidenced in the appearance of cloth factories and spinning mills in Reichenberg. The shift from home- to factory-based working was large-scale. Around the turn of the century, the Ginzkey family had developed a high quality carpet and blanket factory, the largest company in Maffersdorf and known well beyond the borders of Bohemia. In 1906, over 1000 children and as many of the factory's workers welcomed Emperor Franz Josef's arrival by special train into Maffersdorf. The plant housed some 250 perpetually chattering mechanical looms making carpets as large as 12.5 metres wide. In the 1920s, the largest carpet in the world was made there for the

---

[4] Source: Porsche Great Britain copy – Edited (see p.280)

Waldorf Astoria hotel in New York (though this claim was overtaken many years later when the factory went on to make even larger ones to adorn the grand German Reich Chancellory opened in Berlin by Hitler in January 1939).

The factory's prosperity is reflected in the vast family mansion on the upper side of the main road, together with the house at the gate of the mansion, where Marjorie and Gustave lived after their reunion, and in which their daughter was born.

Gustave, then, had grown up in a culture shaped by years of hard work, enterprise, thrift and musical endeavour, coupled with a sharpened appreciation of appearance. His parents nurtured high expectations of their family. Karli played the cello and Gustave the piano to a professional standard. In adolescence, the boys saw a new world opening up before them, with revolutionary modes of transport offering travel opportunities previously reserved for the privileged few.

The Great War intervened when Gustave was fourteen. Unlike Marjorie's father Will, this family had no reason to stay at home. None of the boys was exempt from conscription; after completing his studies, Gustave experienced the effects of the carnage when he served in the army from March to November 1918. Three quarters of the eight million conscripted men in the Habsburg army became casualties, the highest ratio among the warring nations. Gustave's eldest brother Albert was killed, leaving a young wife and child, and Karli was injured. A touching photograph of Karli with seven fellow survivors, taken in the Reserve Spital Leitmoritz dated 20.9.18 conveys the bonds forged in the trauma and loss of war, with the caption *Zum treuen Angedenken*,

Euer Bruden, Karli [in faithful memory, your brother Karli].

Those four years of war played a powerful part in the formation of Gustave's character. The disorientation and soul-searching in terms of his own ideologies caused him much turmoil. He came face to face with Bolshevism through his fellow students and compatriots in the Habsburg peasant army and reserve units. While certainly a socialist, he was no revolutionary; Gustave was more than happy to conform to the social norms he had grown up with. Thus, the reactionary forces in the country at the time were to some degree aligned with his own family values of enterprise, respectability and the desire to improve one's lot in life. This last quality in particular had struck a chord with a certain young Englishwoman; in fact, it was common to the three eldest of Lily's girls.

Gustave had spent most of the Great War years at the Reichenberg Handels Akademie [Business School], where he learnt eight languages on top of his business studies and also took a leading part in a student fencing group which suited his agility. Throughout this period he became still more accomplished at the piano, which he used for his own pleasure and later to entertain his friends.

By the end of the Great War, Gustave had travelled further and met more people from different backgrounds than his parents had in all their sixty years. This experience introduced him to a new kind of kinship, as well as the opportunity to put into practice the language skills for which he discovered he had a special gift.

Paris enabled Gustave to indulge his taste for the finer things in life: he was groomed with Pinaud's Eau de Portugal, breath freshened with Vademecum, and always cloaked in the masculine tang of the cigarettes he smoked.

A meticulous man in his work, he paid great attention to detail. His correspondence illustrates the considerable effort he put into his relationships.

Once demobilised, Gustave worked for a short period at the Sanatorium Frankenstein in Rumberg and then from 1920 to 1922 was employed at the firm of Ludwig Friedrich in Gablonsk, where he lived for some time with the Feizl family. This had been arranged by his sister Mariechen's husband Rudolf Scheifler, an upright, solidly built and taciturn man who was a Maffersdorf jeweller and clockmaker. On a card bearing a picture of the couple with their two children and dog, his hostess wrote to Rudolf on 6th October 1922 letting him know that Gustave had left them for London:

> In Farewell
> A friendly souvenir on the occasion of the departure of our faithful friend Gustl who has become very dear to us, and whose exceptionally great love brought us many pleasant hours. Feizl family.

Gustave came from a respectable and hardworking rural household. His parents, Josef Lange and Anna Panitschka, had both been born in the village of Maffersdorf, about five kilometres from Reichenberg, in 1858 (a whole generation before Will and Lily). He a weaver and she a seamstress, they were married on 18th May 1881 and Gustave arrived nineteen years later, the last of five children, when Anna was 42. By then, his eldest brother was a young man, Mariechen around ten years old, Willi nearly eight and Karli two. As late babies, the two youngest boys received special attention which nurtured their confidence. Gustave and Karli were very close and both loved Mariechen – little Marie – who had looked after them when they were small. Anna Lange worked all her married life to add to the family's income.

The solid three-storey house with the tall pump outside gave the family a certain standing in the village. Josef played the clarinet in a small band which, in great demand, provided fees to assist his determination to own the house in which they lived – an aim he achieved only a couple of years before he died in the mid-1930s. Anna's skills gave her children clothes that were tailor made; thus Gustave's lifelong sartorial elegance had begun early.

Photo dated 26 February 1923 – Anna Lange (centre) and friends

Gustave's aspirations to make his family proud had always governed his decisions; he now had even more reason to better himself. He couldn't help imagining a time when he and Marjorie might have a family of their own to provide for.

CHAPTER SIX

ANNA AND JOSEF

For generations, young men had married local girls; Gustave knew that any hint of his intention to break with tradition would not be welcome in the Lange household. There had also been, in a suitable local family, a daughter who in his parents' eyes would have made the perfect match for either Karli or Gustl. For many years it had seemed a foregone conclusion that a partnership with one or the other was bound to develop. In their college days, the two boys had been openly competitive for the girl's affections, earning much speculation amongst their elders as to which might be the chosen suitor. Maria-Therese (Feisl) was now married with two young children, but that wouldn't deter his parents from encouraging one or two other good prospects for their son, even if their choice was diminishing.

In the five years since he left home, Gustave had matured into a sophisticated and worldly young man. He had paid one or two return visits during that time, but in some ways he had now outgrown them. Anna and Josef were approaching their seventies and naturally wanted him close by as they reached old age. He knew, though, that it was not the distance or even his absence that would have caused the most recent concern, but Karli's feedback from his latest visit. The subject of a foreign girlfriend must have been raised, along with two pairs of eyebrows.

Mariechen's husband Rudolf had told Gustave's parents the news of his return. Rudolf was a close friend of Glazer and as soon as word of the new vacancy at Ginzkey was out, the elderly couple had asked him to put a word in for 'our Gustl'. Reminded of the young man's talent, Glazer had needed little persuasion. Indeed, he was grateful for the prompt and, feeling very pleased with themselves, his parents had waited in anticipation for the process to take its course.

Gustave arrived by train at Reichenberg and then hopped onto the familiar tram which took him within a few minutes' walk of the family home. When he opened the gate to walk up the path, he saw his mother's beaming face at the window. He hadn't noticed that behind their lace curtains most of the neighbouring houses also had excited faces at their windows.

Suddenly aware of the years since he'd bade them farewell, Gustave wondered how different they would seem to each other. His concern fell away within moments; although the family had grown, no-one had changed. When the door flew open, he was engulfed: Anna and Josef, followed by Karli with his latest girlfriend, Willi and his new wife and Mariechen with Rudolph and their little girl, Liesl.

Feeling as though he was riding into the house on their shoulders, Gustave was jostled indoors. Borne along on a cushion of collective excitement and goodwill, for a moment he wondered why on earth he had hesitated to come. In that second, he strengthened his resolve to make Marjorie his wife. He was filled with the desire to share her with these people he loved, and to be head of his own new little family.

'Gustl, Gustl, Willkommen!' rang through the air, first from his parents and then from the rest of the family in chorus. They fell over each other to give him the best chair, Anna pouring him coffee, followed swiftly by *kuchen* from Mariechen.

'Gustl, I want to introduce you to my wife,' announced Willi.

Karli immediately joined in. 'Gustl, I'd like you to meet Olga'.

'Delighted to meet you both,' replied Gustave, then gasped. 'And who is this little angel?'

'I'm Liesl,' smiled the blonde-haired four-year-old. Mariechen glowed with pride: she had been first to present her parents with a grandchild, who she could now show off to the child's uncle. Mariechen's parents radiated the happiness they felt in having their entire family together again. Their joy was infectious.

Gradually each little family unit took their leave, begging Gustl to call in the next day. He assured them he would and eventually he was alone with Anna and Josef. He braced himself for the test. They bombarded him with questions about London and why he had left there so soon.

'What is so special about Paris anyway?' Josef wanted to know. 'Surely you have gained enough experience by now to settle down back here at home, where you belong?'

Perhaps they were right. Gustave was too tired from the journey and the excitement of the welcome to put up any defence. His parents' voices merging into one, his eyes closing, he gave in to sleep.

A shaft of bright sunlight awakened him the next morning, heralding the cacophony of birdsong outside his bedroom window – a refreshing change from the carriages and motor cars converging outside his Paris apartment. Gathering his thoughts, Gustave vaguely remembered being hustled to his old bedroom the previous night by his mother, amid profuse apologies that they had overtired him with their enthusiasm and chatter.

For a moment he basked in childhood memories, recalling with a smile the scrapes he and Karli used to get into. His mother had always been there, her sewing forever at her elbow, to comfort him when he came home in tears.

It was good to be back. His mind wandered to Marjorie: what would she think of it all? Would she be as devoted a mother as his own? The clatter of the breakfast table being prepared jolted him back to the present and he made his way downstairs.

Gustave kept his promise to visit the other members of the family through that weekend, and after a pleasant few days he had found just enough time to prepare for his interview. That day, he arrived at Ginzkey's Head Office well before the appointed time. To his surprise, his efforts appeared to have been quite unnecessary. Mr Ginzkey's only question was, 'How soon can you start?'

Without pausing for a response, he continued to talk at length about the company and the quality of its product. 'Ginzkey has built a reputation for making the finest carpets and bed coverings. We shall be placing our confidence in you to uphold that reputation right across Europe'.

His words settled on Gustave's shoulders, the weight of expectation suddenly uncomfortably heavy.

'Glazer will tell you all about the terms and conditions and will answer any questions you may have.' Mr Ginzkey stood up abruptly, shook Gustave's hand and, motioning him to the door, added, 'Welcome to Ginzkey'.

Gustave was unnerved. This wasn't in the least as he'd expected. Despite his intention to keep his options open, it appeared there was now no decision to be made. It was cut and dried.

His mind was eased to some extent at the subsequent meeting with Glazer. He was relieved to have time to address the details of the offer which, it transpired, were much more generous than he'd expected. One or two questions were later mimeographed on his return to Paris, but already there seemed little doubt. Life was about to change dramatically.

Anna & Josef were delighted with the news. How soon would Gustl be at home with them in Maffersdorf? He had asked for six weeks to give notice to Arnold Grief and to vacate his flat. Amongst the flurry of plans now being made, Gustave worried about Marjorie's reaction to the news. How would he manage without her? He comforted himself with the fact that this would be his means of saving enough to marry her, even if it would take some time.

This time, the parting from his family was not a dramatic one; they all knew he would be returning soon. However, Gustave knew that the time had come for him to tell them he was in love. The news elicited a chilly response. Questions were fired from every angle; his siblings wished him well, but Anna and Josef couldn't hide their concern. This young woman was a dancer or an actress or some such thing. The picture conjured in their minds at this news was distinctly at odds with their vision of an ideal daughter in law.

As Gustave arrived in Paris on his return, Marjorie was there to meet him at the station. Her initial eagerness to hear all that had happened ebbed away as his news unfolded. She determinedly listened with enthusiasm to his descriptions of the family and the hero's welcome he had received, knowing she must support his decision. Trying to picture herself in the same situation with her own family waiting for her in Southampton, Marjorie felt a pang of homesickness. Her sister Olive was now married with two children of her own. How would they react?

The next few weeks were lost in a flurry of preparation as Gustave packed up his apartment. Arnold Grief had been gracious in response to the news, despite his regret at the loss of a good man. He wasted no time in advertising the vacancy, which was met with a considerable response. Gustave therefore found himself involved in part of the selection process for his successor. Once the right man had been appointed, Gustave was to spend extra time showing him the ropes. This had the unwelcome effect of often keeping him late at the office. Less and less of his precious remaining time was now spent with Marjorie. This was a particular blow to her, as she had recently been quietly worrying about a different problem of her own.

She was still busy with *la compagnie* and still loving her stage work, but Marjorie was increasingly tired and was now in little doubt as to the cause. This hot September day, she felt burdened by the weight of her secret. Her initial concerns had been easier to suppress in the weeks of rushed preparation, but the reality of her situation had now dawned on her. The days of unrelenting exhaustion turned into weeks, now accompanied by increasing bouts of nausea.

This was disastrous timing. She agonised, convinced that once he knew of her pregnancy, Gustave would feel obliged to change his plans and stay with her. But he was too far down the road towards his new life. She had resolved to keep the matter to herself for now, at least until he was safely ensconced in the new job.

Much as she felt the need for comfort and reassurance, Marjorie mentioned it to no-one. Even Nita was unaware. Her private agony was exacerbated by the shame this would bring on her family. Determined not to tell them, at least until she had no choice, she drew comfort from the distance between them.

Before long, though, she knew she must consider the effect this would have on her work. This would now be short-lived. She had managed to save a modest amount of money but doubted it would be enough to support her over the long months ahead. The whole business seemed to cause problems in all directions. Marjorie despaired, but stuck firmly to her decision to say nothing to disrupt the current plans.

The day of their parting came. For the first time, Gustave alluded to his plans for their future, but stopped short of proposing to her. This was partly for fear of a rebuttal, but more due to insecurities about the new job. How could he be sure of supporting Marjorie before he had established himself? At least he could offer her his flat until the lease expired. This gave him some comfort as well as a place to return to, he reassured himself, if things perchance did not work out.

He contented himself for now with promises that he would return for frequent visits. After all, his duties were to include Paris and his secret hope was that he could one day make it his base. 'If only I could wave a magic wand,' he thought, 'and just have all these things behind me, then I would be ready.' He busied himself with the immediate demands of the forthcoming journey.

The moment finally came. At the station, gazing into her eyes, Gustave promised he would be back and would write to her often. 'I love you,' he said. 'I'll never forget about you. So please, please, write to me too and soon we'll be together again. Au revoir, my darling. Au revoir.'

As the train pulled away and Marjorie's fluttering handkerchief faded from view, Gustave slumped down in his seat. The worries he had managed to suppress in the romance of their parting now crowded in once more. The train rattled along, taking him further into the unknown. He stared unseeing out of the smeared window next to him, oblivious to the other passengers who jostled and chatted.

CHAPTER SEVEN

BABY GRAHAM

Weighed down by emptiness as well as her secret, Marjorie left the station and made her way back to his lonely apartment with a heavy heart. She must now face life without him; soon, also without the work she loved. Quite how she was going to continue, she could barely contemplate. She did arrange to see a doctor, who confirmed her condition and gave her a date for the baby's arrival in mid-May. Now, in October, it seemed a lifetime away. How would she possibly cope with the months ahead?

She remembered her mother and the relentless succession of babies, one after another. 'Is this what I'm destined for, after all?' she thought tiredly. It felt as though the years in Paris had suddenly been swept away; the future now seemed a gloomy prospect with nothing but poverty and struggle. She knew through backstage gossip that some girls had found help to terminate their pregnancies, but her mind reared away from the very thought. Abortions were illegal; the idea of breaking the law frightened her far more than any possible risk involved. In any case, her conscience simply would not allow her to end a new life. No, she could never do it.

Marjorie felt quite sure that Gustave would never allow it either, but how quickly her own dreams and career were to be over. Feverishly turning over her options in her mind, she tried to imagine how she would cope. She would have to, somehow. Gustave was a good man. He would look after her and their child; perhaps after all, her own career would not be halted forever.

Still far from easy with the situation, she gradually became calmer. She would think of something, try to find different roles once they were settled.

The doctor had advised her not to continue with any strenuous activities; she knew this applied to her dancing and began to wonder what the Hendersons would say. They were worldly people and had always been so supportive. She had little doubt that they would try and accommodate her for the next few months at least. Having considered all her options, Marjorie made a decision. Olive would know what to do. She hastily penned a letter to her sister, pouring out her worries and begging her not to tell another soul.

George and Alice Henderson had already seen the change in Marjorie and knew the signs. This was by no means the first occasion of its kind they'd had to deal with, yet this time they felt personally involved. When she'd joined them she'd been little more than a child. The Hendersons had played a significant part in her development, taking great joy from watching her mature and embrace all the new experiences and challenges their way of life had proffered. While not particularly shocked, they were saddened by the news. They agreed privately that they could foresee the dramatic effect this would have on Marjorie's future probably more clearly than she could herself.

George and Alice wanted to help. They had grown to know Gustave quite well and liked him, so felt particularly anxious about his untimely departure. They urged Marjorie to inform him of the situation, convincing her first and foremost of his right to know, but also his duty to share in the responsibilities that lay ahead.

She was grateful for their concern, but didn't doubt his commitment to her. Having made the decision to have the baby, her unwavering confidence in him reinforced the decision to delay telling him for a little longer. His career, after all, was of paramount importance to any future they might have together. If he knew, he would drop everything to be by her side, so she remained convinced of her plan. 'Far better,' she thought, 'to take time to plan the way forward and be in control of the situation. When he is more settled in the job we will be able to tackle the news much more rationally'.

This determination was vindicated when Gustave's first letter revealed that he was far from happy and missing her dreadfully. She knew that she'd been right to spare him any added worry. However, soon afterwards he wrote inviting her to meet him in Zurich during his first business trip. They could celebrate her 21st birthday together.

As the train rumbled along toward the Swiss border, she thought carefully about how to present the news. She was a little afraid of his reaction but knew she must urge him to continue with the new job. Logistically, marriage would present difficulties because neither of them were French citizens. Either he would have to move to

England or she would have to go to Czechoslovakia, where in any case there was a civil requirement for one party to be resident in the country for at least six months. Neither of them qualified.

He was there at the station to meet her. His embrace told her clearly how much he had missed her and in those few moments her fears evaporated. The weeks since they had parted seemed a lifetime to both of them and their happiness at being together again seemed to be the perfect atmosphere to break the news.

Once back in his little hotel room, Marjorie was finally able to tell him the secret that she'd carried so cautiously for so long. Gustave's initial surprise soon gave way to delight once he was reassured about her wellbeing. Any fears he may have had were well disguised. 'We will marry and you must come and join me in Reichenberg,' he said without hesitation.

'But you're never there and your parents may not accept me – and they certainly won't understand me, nor I them' she replied. She was well aware that her German speaking skills were about equal to theirs of English. Her mastery of the French language had taken three years to develop; French was her common bond with Gustave.

She went on, 'Hopefully you can apply for Paris to be your base and then we can be together. In the meantime, I want our child to be born in England, to have British nationality. Then I can be close to my family. She'd lost so much time she could have spent with them. Marjorie was now very aware that she needed to renew the bond with her own mother. They discussed their options endlessly but always came back to the same dilemma.

Olive's reply was awaiting Marjorie on her return to Paris and provided great comfort. She urged her sister to come and stay with her and Joe and the children as soon as she wished. Although tempted to accept immediately, Marjorie eventually decided to stay in Paris as long as she could.

Only days after Olive's reply came a letter from Gustave. He had moved on from Zurich to the Hotel du Lac in Lucerne, which he described as:

> … the most beautiful place I have ever seen.
> I had no letter from you saying you arrived safely but I hope you had no troubles and are now occupying my place again.
> I cannot imagine that Venice can be nicer – and thought immediately of you and our honeymoon. What a pity dearest, you cannot be with me and see all this beauty. Without you it is only half as lovely. There is a wonderful lake, not as big as the Zurichsee, but surrounded by the most beautiful buildings, almost all of them hotels, I think. And in the background, huge mountains everywhere. There was the most beautiful sunset today and the lake and mountains in the different colours offered the most wonderful picture. You are right Dearest, when one sees all this beauty, one must believe in a God.
> I do pray and hope so much that God will never leave you but protect you during these most dangerous hours of your life and give you back to me as a gift that I do not even deserve, but which I shall consider and appreciate as a gift from heaven.
> I always pray to God that my love will be sufficient to make you happy for all your life.
> Now that you are away I understand all your suffering. You are far too pure, my angel, and I am not worthy of you. Dearest you must write to me and tell me everything you think and suffer. I want to know and live with you, even when I am far away. I promise you that never shall I be cross but understand and try to console you…

Darling angel you must tell me immediately all you are going to do and you will never forget your promise to have no operation.

On his return to Maffersdorf he sent her a picture of himself dated October '27.

To my dearest little woman in devotion and love
Your husband to be – Gustave
Maffersdorf, October 27

Reassured by these words, she soldiered on for several weeks with support from the Hendersons who gave her lighter duties. Then gradually she confided in her friends.

Nita had guessed her predicament and was relieved to have the chance to offer help at last. Once she had heard Gustave's reaction, she was able to gauge her own response. 'That's wonderful news,' she said. 'You poor soul, why on earth have you kept it to yourself for so long? Don't you worry what others will say. It's not their business and in any case, I'll deal with Jerry and Alex. Bet your life they'll all be quite jealous. I know I am. You lucky girl, especially with Gustave to love you so.'

As Christmas approached Marjorie received, with a mixture of joy and fear, an invitation from Gustave to join him and his family in Maffersdorf. She desperately wanted to accept but by now her shape was starting to change. Crippled by guilt and shame, she couldn't begin to contemplate the reaction of his family to the fact that she was clearly carrying their Gustl's child. She couldn't possibly go.

She reconsidered Olive's offer, but the prospect of burdening her and her little family for five whole months until the baby was due seemed too much. Marjorie decided to stay in Paris for the festive season. At least her sickness had subsided and she was among friends who would include her in their celebration on the big day.

Christmas Day began for her with a visit to the beautiful Sacré Coeur in Montmartre. There she prayed earnestly for their child and their future, and for God to be their guide. Weighed down by the uncertainty which lay ahead, she asked Him to help them through it. That Christmas Day, for the first time, she contemplated becoming a Catholic. She had been raised in the Church of England but knew that Gustave came from a Catholic family and that there would be pressures on him to bring their child up in his faith. She warmed to the idea. Somehow, what little she knew of the disciplines of the

Catholic Church appealed to her. She resolved there and then to find out more about it.

Leaving the church on that cold Christmas Day, Marjorie felt unburdened. It was as though she had handed all her problems to her Maker. She'd made a decision and was clear in her mind that she was no longer alone. As if to reflect this new mood, the sun came dancing through the clouds. All was well once more with the world.

The Hendersons' party was full of fun and chatter, but as the hours went by Marjorie was aware that Christmas Day would never be the same again. She had responsibilities now, but found them strangely exciting. She felt strong and confident: it was good to be alive. Most of all, she felt supported by the decision she had made in church that morning. Her spirits were so lifted by the experience that she turned her back on the festivities for a while, looking for a quiet corner of the house in which to be alone.

Marjorie was aware of a curious contentment as she felt the new life stir within her for the very first time. Then, something even more wonderful. She heard her name being called from the other room. George burst in brandishing a telegram from Gustave. He would be arriving by train the next day.

Two days later they committed themselves to each other privately before God in the same church which had given Marjorie such comfort on Christmas morning. Only this time it was late at night and there was no official service. Kneeling in the front row before the altar, they whispered their vows to each other, oblivious to the two people praying in silence at the back of the church. Their short time together was filled with happiness as they indulged one another with fantasies about prospective parenthood. The shared novelty of it all reinforced their bond. Both deliberately suppressed their anxiety about the separation soon to be forced upon them in the firm belief that it would be short-lived.

When they bade each other farewell at St. Lazare for Gustave's very long journey on 29th December, they promised to be in their respective churches at midnight on New Year's Eve to pray together, and so they were.

Marjorie finally made the ferry trip to Southampton a month later. Olive, now expecting her third child, was there to meet her with her two little ones and as they climbed aboard the bus to Totton, Marjorie felt glad to be home. They had so much to talk about, so much lost time to make up for. Their conversation was interrupted only by the bus conductor and the demands of toddlers, too young to understand their grandparents' rule about being seen and not heard.

Both blessed with their father's sense of humour, the two girls spent fun-filled weeks amidst much laughter in those final months of Marjorie's waiting. Olive and Joe were seeking to move, so much of the girls' time was spent house hunting. Marjorie enjoyed sharing in this; privately, it was important to her that when he visited, Gustave should see them in the setting for which Marjorie had prepared him – one which would not reflect the poverty of her childhood.

Belmont was a real find. A detached country house in Ashurst on the edge of the New Forest, it was perfect. Although it was far too expensive, they could just afford it by taking in paying guests. The high ceilings and spacious rooms gave the sisters a perfect canvas on which to paint their vision of English gentility. Olive had a particular gift for transforming the simplest pieces of furniture into enviable antique treasures. They couldn't wait to get their hands on the house. Olive's husband Joe was rather daunted by the prospect, but a double dose of sisterly persuasion eventually gained his approval.

On 28th April, Gustave wrote to Marjorie from Frankfurt-am-Main. He was triumphant: he had his visa and expected to be with her around the 8th to 10th May. The letter closed with:

> Goodnight Dearest, and God bless you and keep you brave until we meet so soon –
> With love, Your Gustave
> My next address:
> Hotel Monopole, Dusseldorf
> or if you post by air mail to Cologne Hotel Minerva

A couple of weeks later Marjorie went into labour. She had booked a bed in a private nursing home in Bishops Waltham, a pretty small country town in the Meon Valley in the heart of Hampshire.

She was grateful to have Gustave by her side during the long hours of her labour, but it was out of the question for the husband to be present at the actual birth. Instead, at the appropriate point, he was escorted to a waiting room.

Marjorie was attended by Nurse Toise, the local district nurse and midwife, and assisted by an auxiliary nurse.

Outside in the waiting room, Gustave quailed at the thought of her suffering. He had been warned that first labours were rarely easy. Of course the staff would use all their experience to help, but what an ordeal for her. If only he could endure it in her place. He paced and smoked cigarettes for what seemed like hours until finally, the door was flung open. 'Mr Lange, you have a baby boy.'

Overjoyed, Gustave hurried in to meet his son and see his wife. Born on 21st May 1928, their newborn son was named Graham Gustave. The young couple were ecstatic to be a family of three.

For Marjorie, Bishops Waltham was perfect. It was close enough to Southampton to be near the family, but far enough away from the city to enjoy the sweet air and green grass of the English countryside.

Spring was now in full flow. Gardens had been transformed from dank wastelands into organised plots ablaze with life and colour.

With time on her hands during the final weeks of her pregnancy, Marjorie had watched the seasons change with newfound interest: first the carpets of white snowdrops gave way to sunny primroses and daffodils, then the magical haze of bluebells greeted her ventures into the New Forest.

The grey backdrop to a skyline of leafless, seemingly lifeless trees and hedges had suddenly become blue. Warmth from the new sunshine had coaxed the scene into vivid life. A splash of pink and white almond blossom amidst the variety of greens adorned the avenue of trees which formed part of Marjorie's daily walk.

She wondered frequently how on earth she could have forgotten the beauty of this land, so different even from the loveliness of Paris and Montmorency.

Now, for ten glorious days they had been a family. They had abandoned themselves to each moment of happiness surrounding the arrival of their little son.

The family had all rallied round; their excitement had masked the inevitability of the new father's imminent departure. Several weeks later Marjorie sent him this photograph as a postcard.

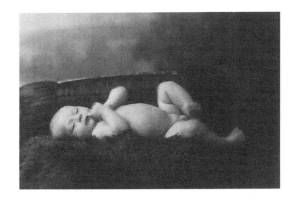

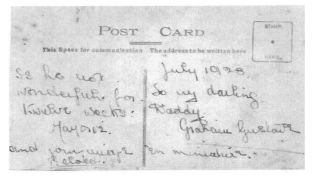

July 1928 To my darling Daddy – Graham Gustave
Is he not wonderful for twelve weeks – Marjorie
And your image en miniature – Beloved

CHAPTER EIGHT

SEPARATION BEFORE MARRIAGE

When the time did come for Gustave's return to Europe, it brought with it endless debates about marriage. Their conclusions were always the same: Marjorie resisted his pleas for her to return with him to Maffersdorf. He left England and his loved ones with great sadness, resolving one day soon to change her mind.

On A. Ginzkey continuation paper, in the Autumn of 1928, Gustave wrote to her in French saying:

> ...I am wondering how you speak English nowadays. In any case you will find my pronunciation very bad since I am no longer in the habit of speaking much. My dear, dear love, what are you doing at this moment? Walking in the garden with your Rudyard [Kipling] or thinking of your Gustave who adores you. And if you could stay there until this evening, we would then go to the Bois to place a beautiful rose on the spot where I confessed my love to you for the first time. My great love, I have often been there this summer...

She was lucky that Gustave sent her regular funds; many girls, she knew, might have been content simply to enjoy life with their baby, but Marjorie's thirst for independence was relentless. She was well aware of his situation and wished fervently that she could make her own contribution. She hated the idea of being a 'kept woman', but at the same time couldn't bear the idea of giving up her son. Marjorie had greatly appreciated Olive's support through the pregnancy, but she knew she could not continue to burden her and Joe.

On the Hampshire coast. Marjorie with Graham, summer 1929

Graham outside Welch's Stores

Marjorie knew that most babies born out of wedlock were given up for adoption, but for her this was out of the question. In her heart she was married; it was only a matter of time before God would bring them all together.

She managed to find a few rooms to let in the village of Pennington, where her regular forays to the local grocery store soon presented a solution. Marjorie had befriended and confided in Mrs Welch, whose husband ran Welch's Stores and who always paid such charming attention to little Graham. To Mrs Welch, this young mother was to be admired – she defied all conventions. Even while pushing the pram, thought Mrs Welch approvingly, Marjorie carried herself with elegance, not to mention an irrepressible energy. Far from appearing downtrodden, this girl seemed to fizz with life.

She often invited Marjorie into her home for a cup of tea. 'Such a lovely baby! I'd be so happy to have him if ever you need anyone.'

This suggestion was a great help. It started with the odd afternoon when Marjorie managed to find a few hours of office work. Graham seemed quite content to stay with Mrs Welch for a few hours at a time. Marjorie's yearning for Paris and the life she'd left behind grew stronger than ever. It seemed natural to discuss her predicament with this lady.

Mrs Welch had developed a great affection for the child and offered without hesitation to look after him. She was delighted at the prospect, which was welcomed by her husband on condition that she would be paid for the pleasure. With everyone in agreement, matters were written down and agreed by both parties so that nothing was left to chance.

Barely five months old, Graham was now safely ensconced with Mrs Welch. His mother made her way back to Paris, looking forward to joining her old friends but most importantly being closer to Gustave. She knew she had a far greater chance of seeing him on that side of the Channel. Europe was his marketplace and the show would take her on tour again. This meant there would be times when they'd be only a train journey apart. It came as a great surprise when she learned she would accompany the show to America. Gustave wasted no time in visiting her before this great adventure. A week later from the Hotel Marquardt in Stuttgart, he wrote:

> ...I am thinking that last Saturday at this minute we looked out from that café and went to the cinema. How beautiful when you put your head on my shoulder. And tomorrow will be worse. How I wish I could just fly to you and stay with you until Monday morning...but perhaps I too might be caught in the rain. Perhaps I was to find you with some apple liking man, or lover unknown until now and so I think I better be not caught in the rain and wait for a better chance.
>
> Dearest, one more week and you will go far, I wish I had some real business over there and could take you with me. I think it is unjust, but can I help it? Wouldn't it be a dream? But I am so confident about you. You will get on splendidly, make nice friends and unhappy boys but you won't after all forget your husband-to-be and *surtout* our beautiful boy. You will write me nice letters and tell me how glad you will be to come back. And you will think of our future what you think will be the best to do. I too shall work out everything only I am afraid I shall not arrive at anything different as from what I have now.
>
> I do hope this money will enable you to get the things you need and when you come back with your $ check book and with plenty of nice things – don't forget my present

for heaven's sake, it seems such an age somebody made me one. We shall make a weekend or longer appointment and talk things over...

That same month the German dirigible Graf Zeppelin made its first commercial flight across the Atlantic, but this was only for the elite. It carried twenty passengers with a crew of forty. This was far out of the Hendersons' reach, their only choice was to cross the Atlantic by sea, a far more drawn-out affair.

Their long-awaited arrival in New York was met with one problem after another. The jazz scene had taken hold and many African American artists were being drawn to New York to take part in Harlem's dynamic jazz and blues music scene. *La petite compagnie Anglaise* found that the venues booked for their performances were shoddy – quite out of keeping with the reputation they had built in Paris. After only one or two performances, the Hendersons booked them all on the next steamer home and Marjorie was back touring the provinces in the build up to Christmas. It had been a very expensive exercise for such a short-lived adventure.

Gustave had been missing her terribly and resolved to make plans for their future. He started to picture their home together, involving himself in window shopping – even selecting the kind of furniture he thought would make Marjorie happy. He wrote to her in earnest from Maffersdorf determined to show her his commitment, spelling out in great detail his plans to have them all together by the middle of the following year and wondering whether his choices of furniture will meet with her approval. The letter written late in 1928 has the first page missing. It reveals his dreams for their future, the underlying fears which have held them both back, and clearly that they will be spending another Christmas apart.

> …It will be summer time for our beginning and you don't know how lovely it is in summer. You can go for wonderful walks with Graham and I shall come home early and meet you somewhere. And whilst I am away you will make our home nicer every week and before it is really winter I shall be back and stay with you again two months over Xmas. I pray so much that you will be proud of our home. I shall love you so and make you forget what those poor people told you in Paris…
>
> I too had a letter from Mrs Welch and those pictures are so wonderful I think I shall adore him, especially when he laughs so much, as Mrs Welch says. My mother too wants to see him very much.
>
> Where do you go on that tour? And where will you stay in four weeks for Xmas? Are you going to think of me when it will be midnight on Xmas Eve? I shall be in thoughts of you and go to Church and pray with you like last year. And you will be *triste, n'est pas* but think that next Xmas we are together and then for ever. Next year we shall already have our Xmas tree with nice presents under it for you and our boy. Then he will be already 19 months – and creep around and make us so much joy. Will it not be wonderful?…And the moment when you with Graham will wait for me at the station or the house will, I swear, be the most lovely in my life. Now tell me that you are not afraid of coming to Reichenberg and that you are happy with me and will do bravely this <u>last</u> thing, go this last *calvario* far from your boy and your Gustave but assisted by his love and appreciation. Six months are very long but when we think that then all our suffering and unhappiness for years will have come to an end…
>
> Good night Beloved, God bless you and watch over you that you remain my good Marjorie until I hold you close in my arms and make you happy as much as I can.

Gustave
The pictures will follow with my next letter. Please write soon.

He wrote to her again from Maffersdorf on New Year's Eve, reflective and a little sad that her letter (he was unaware it was in the post) had been so long in coming:

Dearest Marjorie
I expected this morning to hear from you but in vain. Why do you write now so rarely. Have you so little time? I don't want to let this year pass without telling you for the last time that I love you and hope next year this day, I shall be able to let you feel my love... and make you forget that ever you have been unhappy. I'll try so hard that never shall we disgust ourselves by quarrels and if you will do the same there won't be many people happier than we both with our Graham. He will be nearly two years old and begin to walk and talk and give us a lot of fun. Don't you think all will be beautiful or are you afraid it will not?
Please tell me, as you never do, all your thoughts of the next year and write me soon for I am longing to hear from you.
Yours ever Gustave
My Best Wishes for the New Year!

Marjorie had been at a very low point. The tour had meant that her going home for Christmas was impossible; she had been completely alone – without Gustave and without her baby son. She felt mortified that Graham should be spending his first Christmas with Mr and Mrs Welch. Was this what she had worked so hard to achieve? A powerful combination of guilt and grief made her reluctant to share her feelings with Gustave. His letters had made her strangely fearful; the prospect of living in Maffersdorf filled her with dread.

His reply to hers a week later seems much happier, with talks of arranging a meeting in Switzerland:

> Dearest
>
> When coming home I found your letter on the table. I am so glad and answer at once so that this letter will reach you in Nancy…I told you already that I shall arrange a meeting from Switzerland. If I go to Brussells which is very uncertain yet, I shall of course come to Lille or wherever you are. So you may count that we meet latest beginning of April but possibly before. So to the cadeau that you want to buy for me, it is very sweet of you, but I ask you to keep the money and buy afterwards nice cloth… The news alone that you and baby are well and happy was the nicest present I could receive.
>
> Enclosed please find your picture. I hope you will send it back. I am also glad that you have success. What is it that you play? Is there no dancing to do after the show? Sorry you had such a sad Xmas but it was your own fault if you had no letter, for you had written so little and nothing to say that you would be in Nancy for Noël. I believe you should have had my letter.
>
> With many long kisses
> Love and best sincerest wishes
> Gustave

By April, Marjorie felt as though things were looking up. They had spent a short holiday together, during which time they had turned over and over the impossibility of their situation and come to their usual sensible conclusion that it was best to wait and save so they could afford a real home together. For the time being, they could only think about their next opportunity to meet and arranged a holiday in July. Even so early in the year, they were making plans so that Marjorie would not have to spend another Christmas alone. She had of course asked him to come to Paris for Christmas, but that could only be for a week or more and it would be much more expensive.

When Gustave arrived back on business at the Hotel Metropole in Basel on 11th April en route from Geneva he was still reflecting on their time together. Missing her dreadfully, he could only comfort himself with future plans and dreams; he tried hard to persuade her to think of bringing Graham to join him in Maffersdorf over the quiet winter months. She had managed a fleeting visit to England to see Graham before getting back to the tour.

> Thursday 11th April '29
> My dearest Marjorie
> Only today I have had your first letter sent on to me from Genève. I thank you so much for it. It has made me very happy. I do hope by now that you have received both my letters that I sent to Rouen and that you are at present with our beautiful son. If only you knew how I long for a few lines....Now I am leaving on tomorrow morning and don't think I shall hear from you before Zurich...
> To think that perhaps I shall never see much of our child until he is grown up makes me feel very bitter. Must it not be the most wonderful part where he starts to walk ...Surely it would be nice if you could manage to stay in Paris but don't you think that even those two and a half months from November to the middle of January should be heaven could we spend them together with our angel. And would you not feel unhappy when I should be away from you at Xmas like the past year...
> Love you all
> Your Gustave

They were indeed together for Christmas. It had been a real struggle for Marjorie. The journey to Maffersdorf was long and difficult with little Graham. First she had

had to collect him from his guardians and then take the ferry to Paris, followed by train all the way to Reichenberg via Berlin and Prague. She was so fearful of her in-laws, especially with all the language difficulties they had to face. But she owed it to Gustave to be there and he had convinced her that his parents were longing to meet her and especially their grandson. Marjorie was determined to brave it, for him – it was only for 10 days and they would soon pass.

Gustave alone was at the station to meet them and had arranged a taxi to take them the last three miles from Reichenberg to Maffersdorf.

Anna and Josef were at the door in no time as they saw the taxi pull up outside. There was great excitement in the house. The formal introductions to Marjorie soon gave way to fussing over little Graham, who was exhausted by the journey and bewildered by the attention, not to mention the incomprehensible words coming from so many different faces.

On Christmas Eve presents were distributed after the church service and the preparations for Christmas Day began.

It was all very different to the way Marjorie and her family usually celebrated, but the day itself was joyful as family members arrived with little ones. Willi's daughter Margit was nearly four and took a great interest in little Graham, always under the watchful eye of cousin Liesl who had reached the grand age of seven.

The children played happily with the small gifts they'd received whilst their parents chatted awkwardly to Marjorie using Gustave as their interpreter.

Marjorie felt, with great relief afterwards, that she had sailed through it in spite of her fears, but she and Gustave were both glad when the day was over. Now they could finally settle down to the business of simply being together.

This was all Gustave had been waiting for since their last meeting in April, but he had not wasted the months in between. He had tried at every opportunity to find somewhere sufficiently smart and attractive to entice Marjorie to come and join him in marriage and set up home. He planned to take her to all the best residential areas around Maffersdorf and Reichenberg and had been doing plenty of window shopping.

Anna, Josef and other members of the family were very happy to act as babysitters for Graham whilst his parents were out exploring.

Gustave took Marjorie to the Slaty Lev [The Golden Lion], the smartest hotel in Reichenberg. She was dazzled by its golden chandeliers and sumptuous carpets: 'Made by Ginzkey, of course.'

Determined to wine and dine his wife, they danced to a jazz band after a delicious meal and he eventually convinced her that she could live happily there. She much preferred the vibrancy of the city to the quiet of the countryside where he had grown up.

By the time she and the baby were due to leave, Gustave had elicited a promise from her that they would have a quiet family wedding in the summer and make this their home.

However, they agreed that there remained one objective on the horizon: a return to Paris, as a family, as soon as Gustave could arrange it with Ginzkey.

The return journey was twice as tedious as the first. Once again, Marjorie felt very alone and for the first time began to question what she was doing in Paris. It was still her favourite place in the whole world, but not without Gustave and her child. The fun had gone out of it and now she really did have to think about Graham. He was growing up and her guilt was growing along with him.

She continued for a short time in order to save a little money for rent on temporary accommodation, and returned to England three months later in May, having bade her last farewell to the company in Paris.

Once home, and after a few days with Olive, Marjorie was pleased to find a little furnished house to rent. She could just afford it for the few months until their departure for Czechoslovakia.

Gustave wrote again on Graham's second birthday.

> Beloved   21st May '30
> I will not let this important date in our lives go by without writing you and telling you that all day long my thoughts have been with you and our beautiful son. Two years old already and to think that both of us, and especially I, have seen almost nothing of him in those two years. When I am going to see him at last, he will already be a little man, quite astonished to see suddenly a new Daddy about him who he is to love all of his life. And to me he will be a little 'cadeau', the book of our beautiful love story in Paris and Montmorency whose pages will make us live again those lovely hours, fill us with happiness and gratitude and leave those lives empty where the bitterness of our sufferings wanted to destroy all the beauty, tear our hearts in two and leave this work unaccomplished...
> And I am happy to hear from you the same day that this great love is still in your heart and can fill your eyes with tears...
> How is our son? I hope in best health and happy to be with his real Mama. I wish I could have sent him a nice <u>cadeau</u> for today but as so soon I shall be with him, I must see the joy in his eyes and heart, it just would not be the same. I hope you will have given him a nice day in your

new home and you will have told him of his Daddy, that so soon he is coming to bring something very nice for his boy. It will be one of my happiest moments when I can meet you both and when you take me to your house. I pray to God that he will keep you both in best health until then and that we shall have sunshine and peace…

God Bless you. Write soon and answer my questions. Goodnight Dearest. I love you both and wished I could come to you tomorrow morning.

Thousand Kisses, Your own Gustave

When he arrived there was great rejoicing. His stay was just long enough to meet Olive and Joe and thank them again for all their support.

They discussed their wedding and decided to keep it very low key. There would be a formal registration ceremony and Gustave's family would all rally round to produce the wedding breakfast.

Marjorie was happy with this, feeling guilty that her own family could not be there and, in any case, preferring to keep the costs down so that funds could be stretched to set up their home together.

Just over two months later they were finally married in Reichenberg on August 4th 1930, surrounded by Gustave's family and with little Graham in attendance. The festivities continued, in less formal attire, at a separate family celebration.

Separation Before Marriage

Wedding Day, Civil Ceremony, 4th August 1930

CHAPTER NINE

PARIS & THE DEPRESSION

The Langes became a real family when they moved to their first home, an apartment on the first floor of a large, elegant house in Reichenberg, Czechoslovakia[5]. This was a prosperous neighbourhood; the house was set in spacious floral gardens intersected by pathways that invited exploration. Marjorie and Gustave at long last had the chance to spend more time together with their son as a family, but financial hardship was soon to follow.

---

[5] Now Liberec, Czech Republic

As the recession turned into the Great Depression, countless businesses suffered unemployment, unimaginable inflation and economic ruin. Ignaz Ginzkey, Gustave's employer survived, but only just, due at least in part to the prudence of its management. His correspondence refers to a letter written to Gustave in 1931 by his Personnel Manager and personal friend, in which he affirms the Directors' appreciation of his work, while regretfully informing him that they could no longer pay his full salary.

Business had come to a standstill and workers had to be laid off. They offered him the option of seeking alternative employment or remaining on the staff on restricted terms for an estimated period of six months until, it was hoped, the economy would begin to recover. As soon as the financial situation permitted, they would not only resume his salary but also seek to reimburse him to some extent for the loss of income. Gustave chose to stay on.

By February, an apologetic letter from Ginzkey shows just how serious things were: the majority of workers were now redundant and the small remaining office staff were faced with a further salary reduction. Ginzkey once more reiterated his hopes that the situation would soon ease and that trading would resume at the proper levels. However, another letter followed three months later:

I. GINZKEY MAFFERSDORF,
MAFFERSDORF-PRAGUE-BRNO-KARLSBAD

12 May 1932
Mr. Gustav Lange, Maffersdorf
You too must now be aware that the crisis in the world economy is getting worse day by day and the effects are

also becoming ever more severe in Czechoslovakia. Recently the various increases in the rates of import duties and the banning of imports into countries which were previously regular customers for our firm's products have now taken away from me the last possibility of keeping a worthwhile export market going.

As no end to these catastrophic circumstances can be foreseen at the moment, and under the pressure of exceptional circumstances, which unfortunately it is not in my power to avoid, I find myself obliged with a heavy heart to give notice today that on 30th June you are released from your service agreement with my firm.

Hard as this decision may seem for you, it is equally hard for me, although I confidently hope that this situation is only temporary, and I will soon be in a position to recall you to take up your post with us once more.

Whatever happens, please do not become discouraged but carry on your duties as keenly as before in the expectation that eventually and in the end healthy common sense must sooner or later break through and restore the world economy, and this desperate situation will give way to healthier circumstances.

Yours faithfully,
Signed J Ginzkey

Their happy family had to endure another separation after all too short a time together. Marjorie was forced to return to Paris just to make ends meet, enrolling Graham in a kindergarten. Their letters were a lifeline to them both; a letter dated 1931 from Reichenberg contains the remark, 'tomorrow is again letter day'.

Hope began to surface eventually. A report written by Gustave states that the factory in Maffersdorf was back in production while many industries were still at a standstill. 'While he would not be surpassing last year's turnover, the following year should be much better' he wrote.

Things did improve significantly later that year when Gustave was appointed permanent representative for the new House of Ginzkey for Scandinavia, Belgium, France and North Africa. Full of optimism, Ginzkey set themselves the goal of achieving leadership in their field by producing goods of the highest quality and design. They boasted the use of the most modern technology, using the widest carpet loom in the world. In addition to the Waldorf Astoria Hotel in New York, Ginzkey carpets were made to order for the world's largest opera houses.

Gustave and Marjorie achieved their long-held dream when they finally moved to Paris, where he established his office at the end of 1932. They found an apartment in the prestigious 16th Arrondissement and Marjorie bought furniture in England, which she arranged to be shipped to Paris. Marjorie's career on the stage had now been willingly exchanged for the role of full time wife and mother. She busied herself creating a comfortable home for her husband and son. They were delighted when their happily anticipated second child, James Henry Lange, was born in the British Hertford in Paris at 48 rue Villers, Le Vallois-Perret, on April 30th 1933. The family were now contentedly settled in Paris, with little Graham approaching his fifth birthday.

Their spacious apartment at No 3 rue Verdi was elegant and well-appointed, part of a grand, period property in the sought-after residential area of Paris. Gustave had made significant gains for his Czech employer, who in turn had rewarded him for his success. At last the family were settled following their long separation, although Gustave still needed to travel a great deal. Content with her lot, Marjorie made new friends.

Maria Sanson was an English woman from Liverpool married to Pierre. She became Marjorie's closest friend. Her two children were close to Graham in age and the two families spent many happy hours together. Near to their home was a park in which Marjorie and the boys spent a great deal of time.

Gustave's career was in its ascendancy. Those few years were so successful that the family was able to move to a brand new, stylish apartment in Neuilly near the Bois de Boulogne. It was the height of contemporary 1930s chic; they were the envy of their friends. Marjorie had never been happier.

During these golden years, very aware of her good fortune, Marjorie made a trip home to visit her parents. She knew that, in stark contrast to her own situation, they were struggling to make ends meet.

CHAPTER TEN

SEVERN BEACH OR RIVA BELLA?

Marjorie was nervous about her visit home. She would have to witness first-hand the indelible mark left on the working classes by the depression. Southampton's shipyard had laid off many men, including her own father. The prospect of work in Avonmouth had prompted a move to an address, at The Bean Acre, in Shirehampton. Some years later they had moved once more, to the tiny village of Severn Beach, just four miles along the Severn Estuary.

Marjorie's sisters had also now left home, so Will and Lily arrived in Severn Beach with their two youngest sons, now in their early teens. With just enough funds for the first few weeks, they rented a little bungalow in Beach Avenue. She looked forward to seeing her daughter and hearing about her life in Paris. It seemed impossibly glamorous to Lily.

Marjorie's visit was timely. Seeing her family sharing such a small space, she was troubled by the comparison with her comfortable life in Paris. She was deeply concerned about her parents' finances and how they would cope, but during her visit an opportunity arose for them to buy their rented house at a very good price.

Marjorie was very keen for them to have the security of their own home; she helped them with the deposit and committed herself to a significant monthly contribution towards the mortgage payments. Marjorie's Socialist upbringing still tugged at her conscience. She was glad to have been able to help, but kept the arrangement secret from Gustave; his thrifty nature would undoubtedly raise objections.

For some time, she managed to keep up these payments by using her clothing allowance, but in 1937 the franc devalued considerably. The exchange rate now made it almost impossible for her to maintain the payments. Marjorie realised that a contingency plan was essential if she was to avoid getting into trouble with Gustave.

The only way to financial independence, Marjorie decided, was to start one's own business. She persuaded her mother to come for The Paris Exhibition which opened that summer. They enjoyed a precious week together and when her mother offered to take Graham back to England for a short holiday no mention was made of financial concerns. Instead she welcomed the opportunity to work on a solution.

Her worries about Graham's welfare and conduct were somewhat assuaged by a contract written by Gustave for Graham to sign before he left:

> *I have promised my mother on my word of honor <u>not</u> to get up in the morning even to go to the bathroom, before the breakfast is on the table, to dress myself properly and to go to bed every night at 7.30 punctually. Also I promise faithfully never to touch a*

fire or to go <u>too</u> near the sea and always to tell Grandma where I am when I go out.
   Graham Lange

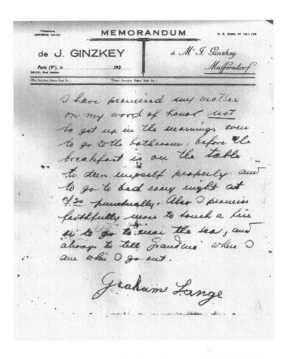

When it was announced that the Paris Exhibition was extended for another year, she seized on the idea that surely the vast number of visitors from all over Europe would support a *salon de thé* right in the centre of Paris?

Bursting with enthusiasm for her plan, she couldn't wait to share it with Gustave. Oblivious to the reasons for her new-found ambition, he agreed to give her £100 towards the venture. This still left her short of the £125-140 she needed to start up. She wrote to her father's sister Aunt Liz, explaining at length that she was not asking for a gift or handout, but offering her Aunt a 10%

share if she would be willing to invest £40 in this venture. She stressed that this would enable her to keep up the contribution towards her parents' mortgage. 'Gustave would be willing to give me the full amount,' she wrote, 'but this would mean it would be his business and not mine'.

The *salon de thé* did not materialise, but her ambition of running her own business remained. Long summer weekends spent on the Normandy coast at Riva Bella, a little place near Caen, inspired Marjorie with visions of running a guest house.

She longed for the chance to put her own mark on something and make a real success of it, but it took a further two years for her to persuade Gustave, by which time their lives were about to change dramatically.

Most Sudeten Germans had been content to remain part of Czechoslovakia until Adolf Hitler came to power. However, in 1935 the Sudeten-German Party, financed by Nazi Germany, had begun to complain that the Czech dominated government discriminated against them. Germans who had lost their jobs in the depression began to argue that they might be better off under Hitler.

The Sudetenland contained nearly all Czechoslovakia's mountain fortifications. No longer able to defend itself against further aggression, it was only a matter of time before the whole of Czechoslovakia was under German occupation. In September 1938 Neville Chamberlain, the British prime minister, met with Hitler at his home in Berchtesgaden. Hitler threatened to invade Czechoslovakia unless Britain supported Germany's plans to take over the Sudetenland.

After discussing the issue with the French and Czech leaders, Chamberlain informed Hitler that his proposals were unacceptable. However, this decision was reversed at a conference in Munich later that month when, desperate to avoid war and anxious to avoid an alliance with Stalin and the Soviet Union, the British and French premiers agreed that Germany could have the Sudetenland. In return, Hitler promised not to make any further territorial demands in Europe. On 29th September the Munich Agreement was signed, transferring Sudetenland to Germany.

The German army marched into Sudetenland on 1st October, 1938. Gustave's heart sank at the news. Born to an Austrian father and Slovak mother, overnight he faced the prospect of becoming a German national.

It was a far cry from the two weeks in August 1936 when Berlin hosted the Olympic Games, recalled Gustave. Adolf Hitler had dazzled many foreign spectators and journalists with an image of a peaceful, tolerant Germany. Marjorie too had been swayed, but Gustave had many Jewish friends and remained resolutely anti-fascist.

He felt reluctant to face up to the risk of this new-found, unwanted status and when later given a choice he chose to remain Czech. Nevertheless, he felt safest in Paris and in his travels to the Northern lands. Almost to reassure himself that his misgivings were unfounded, he gave Marjorie his blessing to buy the lease on Le Rayon de Soleil, a large and very pretty house in Riva Bella. They also bought a plot of land there, discussing the possibility that as property owners they might now be given a foothold into French citizenship.

Marjorie was now able to realise her long-held dream of running her own business. The guest house ran well for the summer of 1939. Mona came to help and their teenage brother Terry visited too. He soon became infatuated by the glamour of a much older sister and her life in France. They also employed a governess/ nanny for James, Katya Goriakov, who quickly became a friend and remained so for many years.

Graham had found a new interest in horse-riding and rather welcomed his mother's preoccupation with the hospitality business. She was happy for him to spend many long hours at the stables, where he was learning to ride as well as helping with the mucking out and other general chores. He became an accomplished rider and put the horses through their paces, nurturing an ambition to become a jockey.

Le Rayon de Soleil, Riva Bella

CHAPTER ELEVEN

WAR CLOUDS...THE FOREIGN LEGION

Marjorie's guest house ran for less than one summer. When Adolf Hitler's early success as Chancellor in Germany had elevated him to hero status with his promises of a bright future for all, much of Western Europe was initially swayed by his apparent charisma.

But now, the threat of war in Europe had been growing for months and while Gustave had not shared his wife's earlier optimism about Hitler, he still felt reluctant to face up to the signs that trouble loomed.

For a while, he felt comparatively safe in France. But as time went on, Gustave was aware of increasing unease and became more and more concerned for his wife and young family. The advancing threat was becoming ever more real. He now understood that if war was declared between Britain and Germany, he could still be called up to fight with the Germans against his wife's people.

Whilst Marjorie was busy that summer at Riva Bella, Gustave spent many sleepless nights, either in Paris or on his travels, pondering his dilemma. He simply must do whatever he could to gain French nationality. Having lived for so long in Paris, it felt natural that he should be

French; he had taken the first step in showing that commitment by investing in Riva Bella, but when it became apparent that France was allying itself to Britain, the solution came to him in a flash. If war was declared, he would volunteer for the French Army. This would reinforce his commitment to France and his aim to acquire a French passport. Gustave did not realise then that the authorities would disagree; living and working in France alone would not be enough.

When he finally told his wife of his plan, Marjorie was horrified. Surely at 39 years of age he could not compete with the fitness of young conscripts? She hoped they would turn him down and allow him to join the Resistance movement. But when the reality of his position was fully explained to her, she was powerless to argue. The alternative would be for Gustave to go back to Maffersdorf and face the risk of being called up to fight for Germany: a prospect too awful to contemplate and completely out of the question.

She too had been reluctant to face the prospect of war – France was her home now and she felt very safe. She loved her life between Paris and Riva Bella and did not want to give it up. She also worried about uprooting Graham. His keen interest in the local training yard for racehorses had occupied him for most of the summer. He was settled and happy there and the opportunities they gave him for an occasional ride were increasing week by week, along with his dream of becoming a jockey.

She simply couldn't bear to leave. They had some savings which would keep them going, albeit on a careful budget. Marjorie felt confident they would manage. She begged Gustave to sit tight and stay under cover, but to no avail. He was far too honourable.

On 30th August, 1939 France evacuated 16,000 children. Graham and James were not in their number, but a picture postcard addressed to her mother from Neuilly on Seine in Mona's handwriting and stamped 29th August 1939 shows that she was visiting Marjorie at that critical time. Mona writes that the crossing had been good and they have arrived safely, and Marjorie added a postscript: 'Jim is marvellous'.

Only two days later on 1st September 1939 Germany invaded Poland; so began World War II. Two days after that, Britain and France declared war with Germany, and on that same day Marjorie took the boys back to Paris for a very important reason. On 4th September James acquired French nationality *par declaration devant M. le Juge d'instance de Neuilly*[6] – Marjorie had been determined to ensure that at least one of her family was officially recognised as French. She felt a quiet pride in her skill at dealing with the authorities. Surely it would all be over soon.

The following day Gustave presented himself as a volunteer conscript to the French Army but there was a lot of suspicion at that time that it was being infiltrated by foreigners and spies, so he was instead referred to the Centre for Special Engagements to the Foreign Legion where he registered on 5th September 1939. The Foreign Legion did not insist on French nationals. Gustave still hoped this would help his case for becoming a French subject, though he did not expect that it would take him to another continent; so far away from his wife and family.

Although he had registered in September, he was not called up for service until 10th November, 1939, the date

---

[6] By declaration before the Magistrate

on which he officially enlisted as a volunteer for the duration of the war.

The bigger shock came when he boarded a military plane with people of mixed nationalities and with a much less refined outlook and background than his own; indeed, often at each other's throats. Foreign regiments provided refuge for many who wanted anonymity.

He found that flight to be extremely daunting. Being considerably older than the majority of his company, he wasn't pleased at the attitude of others but, in time, they began to respect his quiet, unassuming presence.

He arrived with his unit in Bel-Abbès, Algeria on 29th November 1939.

The loneliness and homesickness which assailed him when he arrived were almost unbearable. For several weeks Gustave wondered constantly whether he had done the right thing. This was an alien land indeed. Miles and miles of dust, punctuated by dazzlingly white, squat buildings. The sun beat down relentlessly and the fine sand permeated every item of clothing, every belonging. He was grateful for the neck protection his cap provided; many younger fellows learned the perils of sunstroke the hard way.

Gustave watched the comings and goings of local men swathed in light-coloured robes and envied their ability to appear normal in such an environment. The heat of the Algerian desert was an ever-present physical oppression, but what depressed him most of all was the lack of any contact with home. He missed Marjorie and his two sons desperately. There was, at least, a regular supply of cigarettes for the men and this became the smallest of comforts.

Over the following weeks and months, he somehow settled into this strange way of life. The endless drills.

The dust. Of course there was combat but he was spared the front line. This was doubtless due in part to the fact that he was twenty years older than most of his company. However, his gentle nature, attention to detail and excellent language skills were appreciated; Gustave was frequently assigned administrative tasks which required interpretation.

He became a fatherly figure to the younger legionnaires who sometimes sought his counsel. He could be trusted not to break their confidences, especially with the more brash elements of the Corps which formed the vast majority. But even the toughest recruits had their weak moments; Gustave always made time to listen when the need arose.

When the news came through that France had officially surrendered in 24th June, 1940, there was outrage and disbelief in the camp. Morale inevitably dipped but, sustained by the fighting spirit of the men, the Foreign Legion continued to support the Allies.

In spite of a general reluctance to send entire Legion units to France, the French authorities decided something must be done with those loyal elements of the Legion which were still marking time in North Africa. Volunteers were called for and two battalions of 1,000 men each were assembled, one in Morocco in Fez and the other in Sidi bel Abbès. Volunteers for those units were carefully screened; the only Germans permitted to remain in them were veteran legionnaires of unquestioned loyalty. Those men were given new non-German names and false identity papers to protect them in case they were captured[7].

---

[7] Source: www.historynet.com (see p.280)

Though bitterly disappointed, Gustave was not surprised that they were in no hurry to send him home. In any case, what home? It was unbearable to believe that France was occupied by the Germans. What would become of his darling wife and the boys? Gustave was desperate for news of them. He managed to get a sparse amount of mail into Switzerland via the Red Cross, but had no way of knowing whether it reached the family whom he still believed to be in Paris.

As the weeks dragged into months, it became more and more difficult to maintain the calm resignation that had served him so well. Gustave was increasingly restless; six months later, when the news came that he was finally to be demobilised, he could hardly contain his relief and joy.

On 7th November 1940 he was flown back to France, to the non-occupied Vichy zone. He was ecstatic to be back in his chosen home country and there, with the help of the Red Cross, he began the search for his wife and family.

CHAPTER TWELVE

UPROOTED – CAMPS TO MAFFERSDORF

When the first sirens had reverberated through Paris more than a year earlier, Marjorie and Gustave were still together. They had both felt a great sense of unease. Gustave awaited the promised call to arms and Marjorie was dreading not only their separation, but also the void he would leave behind – and in such tense times. Although nervous, she was determined not to let it show. They and most of Paris braced themselves for the unknown. The tension was inescapable; people huddled together in the streets to discuss in hushed tones the latest reports, each arguing their own interpretation of the scant news items.

Some families rushed for the Metro or any underground shelter they could find for cover, but the Langes simply blacked out the windows and held their breath. Before long the all clear came and they realised it was just a test. They both told the boys, 'This means that France and Germany have declared war. We must keep calm. Germany will try and march into France but the Maginot Line is well-nigh impregnable. The French Army has had time to prepare so we will not worry now.'

That first wave of dread and unrest was already settling down by the time of Gustave's departure. Alone without him, Marjorie felt desolate. She sought comfort from her friend Lisa Steinhardt, whose Jewish husband had fled to South Africa with a promise that he would send for her as soon as he could. Lisa waited and waited with her little daughter but the call had not come.

Weeks, then months passed and life for Marjorie and the boys went on much as usual. At first she began to wonder why Gustave had gone. Perhaps it had all been a terrible mistake. Thank heavens she had not sent her boys away with labels around their necks, or indeed joined the many thousands of refugees who trailed endlessly out of the city. Instead, such was her confidence that she enrolled Graham as a weekly boarder into *L'Ecole de St Nicolas* in Buzenval. This Jesuit Catholic school, not too far from Paris, was run by monks.

Gustave's philosophy of saving for a rainy day had certainly come in useful, she reflected now. Although they were not well off, the family would be able to survive, albeit on rations. Life continued much as before, although much to her sadness the guest house had not survived a second summer. There was no tourism to support it, but in most other respects, Paris seemed to Marjorie to be functioning as normal. In England, things appeared to be just the same. People had begun calling it 'the phoney war'.

Then one day in May 1940, just short of Graham's 12th birthday, the first bombs fell over Paris. In fact, Germany had started its offensive with six weeks of air raids over the whole of France before reaching the capital.

The Paris sirens blared on the same day that Graham sat his examination for his Certificat d'Education. He had heard them many times before, but those had merely been rehearsals for this dreaded reality. At home, Marjorie and James donned their gas masks and went down into the nearest shelter while the Luftwaffe droned over Paris like a swarm of bees.

From his desk in the exam room Graham watched in horror as smoke billowed from the direction of their home. This was the first air raid on Paris; he prayed that his mother and brother would be safe.

It was terrifying for Marjorie. She was beside herself with worry about Graham – the poor boy was still at school. Would they be expected to remain in the classroom while bombs fell? Huddled in the shelter, she thought too of her loved ones in England. Were they also experiencing such things? Marjorie wished herself crouched in the bosom of her family rather than in this cold dark shelter, an eternity from home. She thought, too, of the Langes in Maffersdorf. How had she ever come to be in this situation? Her birth family and in-laws were now at war, by default rather than desire of course, but nonetheless it was possible that they might actually have to fight each other. The prospect made her feel faint.

Most of all, she thought of her Gustave in the North African Desert, part of a very different army from the one he had wanted to join. She longed just to hear from him and to seek comfort from him but all to no avail. Marjorie often found herself feeling resentful that she was having to cope with everything on her own. But then she would check herself – what about the thousands of other wives whose husbands were out there fighting and getting killed in this horrible war? What right did she have to feel any different?

When they were able to emerge after the 'all clear' siren was heard, she raced back to their apartment with James as fast as she could. When Graham walked through the door Marjorie burst into tears of relief. They had survived the first air raid.

The Germans invaded France on the ground from the East. They came in through Belgium, circumventing the Maginot Line. Within eight weeks they were marching into Paris. Marechal Petain surrendered, sparing Paris and negotiating a demarcation line which saved half of France the humiliating occupation by German troops. The Armistice was signed on 22nd June 1940 followed by France's official surrender two days later.

Marjorie watched as tens of thousands of Parisians fled the city. Some were killed on the roads by low flying planes or died from other causes. She knew that she had hesitated too long now to leave the apartment and its treasured contents and escape to England. She tried to reassure the boys: 'We will stay, and you will see the Germans are not the Huns which they are believed to be. There are so many good, normal people among them. We shall be alright'.

What did one do in this situation? Marjorie stocked up with dry goods and filled the bath with water. She pulled down the blinds, locked the doors and waited with her boys for the unknown.

One day went by, then another, but all remained uncannily quiet. Gradually, one child's voice could be heard outside, then another and another. The few remaining occupants of the apartments were those whose small businesses were their lifeblood. For very different reasons to Marjorie's, they too had decided to stay.

One morning they looked through the blinds to see German tanks rolling in. Not a shot was heard. After a while a truck stopped near their block and German soldiers got out for a cigarette. Slowly the children appeared, curious to see these strangers. The soldiers offered them sweets and the ice appeared to be broken.

In just a few days the shops opened again and whatever was there was sold. The Germans established places where francs could be exchanged for Deutsch marks, the new currency. Soldiers guarded the few shops whose owners had left. Life seemed to Marjorie to go on nearly as normal.

Eventually, she allowed the boys to go out. They had been cooped up for so long; she hadn't the heart to refuse. They returned shortly after leaving for their first outing, having stumbled across dead bodies beside the river Seine covered with flies. The boys took it in their stride but their mother felt physically sick when they told her what they had seen.

On another occasion, the boys met friendly soldiers whom they invited home, telling them, 'My mother speaks German.' Their block of flats was almost empty: most people had left. German officers inspected the flats and requisitioned them. Officers and personnel enjoyed moving into these lavishly furnished apartments. Before they did, Graham and James managed to get into the flat of a Jewish family whose children they knew. They marvelled at the opulent interiors; it seemed so strange, they whispered to each other, that the family had simply fled, leaving everything just as it was.

It soon became all too clear why. The officers saw no reason why they should allow Marjorie and the boys to remain in their apartment.

'What makes you think *you* are so special?' the Gestapo's voice rang in Marjorie's ears. 'Why should you be allowed to keep your home when all around you have lost theirs? We need these premises. In any case, your husband is wanted by the Gestapo. If you refuse to give him up, then you must be punished and that is that. I'll give you one last chance to tell us his whereabouts.'

Marjorie really did not know where he was. Not that she would have told them if she did, she thought angrily.

By August, the summer heat was taking its toll and the Gestapo stance remained resolute. Marjorie had tried all the charm she could muster; in the end, some new arrivals gave her several weeks to come up with the details of Gustave's whereabouts.

Eventually, they allowed her to stay whilst her case was investigated, on condition that she release two rooms of her apartment for the use of a German NCO called Peter. He was a huge but very gentle man and over the weeks they became friends.

All the inhabitants who remained had to register. Within days everyone was summoned to an address and Marjorie was interrogated. To her astonishment, there seemed little they didn't know about the family. It was all contained in a *dossier*.

First and foremost, they wished to know why her husband, a Sudeten German, had refused German citizen-ship after the *Anschluss*, or Annexation of Czechoslovakia. Why had he joined the French army? She did not correct their assertions, neither of which were technically true. Instead, she replied quite innocently in German: that they had lived in Paris for six years and simply felt more French than anything else. Her explanation fell on deaf ears. Marjorie was informed that she and the boys would have to be interned in a transit camp. Stunned, she protested strongly and managed to get a deferral of two more weeks before they would be required to appear again. She received a stark warning that failure to turn up with the boys for this next appointment would result in them *coming to get her*.

For the next two weeks, Marjorie did a great deal of soul searching. She knew these people were human beings underneath; she could not believe that they would go through with their threat. She resolved to approach them next time in a friendlier manner and appeal to their better natures.

When the day came, she took the boys along. It was an intimidating sight to see men in uniform carrying revolvers, especially after the scene the children had witnessed at the Seine. Marjorie steadied her nerves and, once more, tried to be charming, asking in German what they required of her to avoid internment.

'It is easy', came the reply. 'Just accept your right to German citizenship and then you can stay here with all your belongings. These boys being minors will also be German citizens, irrespective of their place of birth'.

Despite having been at pains to point out that Graham had been born in England and James in France, this was the only response Marjorie received. The soldiers produced some forms which required a great deal of explanation and ordered her to return in another two weeks.

She took the forms just to buy them more time. However, Marjorie privately had no intention of agreeing to German citizenship. Next time, she decided, she would argue that when she married Gustave she renounced her British citizenship and became a Czech citizen. The withdrawal of their passports had deemed her stateless.

Her interviewer was not in a friendly mood on the day of their return and ridiculed her naivety. 'We have been very generous to give you a chance to make good. You, the wife of a man who dishonoured his name and his country'.

Abandoning all attempts at charm, she retorted, 'No. I am an Englishwoman and always will be. I could not contemplate a decision which would lead to my boys having to fight my own brothers. No!'

She tore up the forms in front of them. Graham was terrified. Shaking with fear, he was convinced that at any minute the men would pull out their guns and shoot all three of them.

Her interviewer lost patience. 'You give us no choice,' he snapped. 'You and your children will be repatriated to your Sudeten homeland where you will be a good German citizen. But first you will be moved to a Transit Camp while arrangements are completed. You may go home for now. We will come to take you away.'

Relieved to get out of that place and to breathe fresh air again, they walked in silence to the apartment. Once inside, Marjorie explained to the boys what internment meant: they were to be locked up somewhere and would lose everything they possessed. 'Don't worry', she assured them, 'I will never leave your side and you will be safe with me'.

This had been her biggest dread but she had tried to prepare. She had pleaded with Peter, her Nazi 'house guest', who had promised to do everything in his power to save her the contents of her home[8].

---

[8] He kept his word. Once the family was removed, Peter managed to get the contents of their apartment declared German property and

In the meantime, Marjorie and the boys were taken to a large camp in Vincennes on the east of Paris, where many English people, Australians and Americans were kept behind barbed wire. Marjorie was appalled. The conditions were unbearable. They all slept in one long dormitory on straw. She tore up shirts she had taken so they would have something clean to lay their heads on for fear of fleas and lice. Unable to accept their situation, she complained to the Commandant until he transferred them to another camp.

Their new 'home' was just as bad. Marjorie was unaware that it was nothing short of miraculously lucky that her complaints had resulted in anything other than immediate shooting. Perhaps it was her perfect spoken German, rather than her passionate articulation of their case, which had helped.

Her reaction to their incarceration, like her compatriots', was borne out of exhaustion, anxiety and frustration. Marjorie had lost her beloved home to these infiltrators and after weeks of questioning about Gustave's whereabouts and remaining firm in her story, this felt like the final insult. She wondered if she might as well have spared herself the torture and given in to their demands, at least as far as she'd been able.

She really did know nothing as to the location of Gustave's unit, although she was receiving very infrequent letters via a contact in the Red Cross in Switzerland. She knew that if any cracks appeared in her claims for complete ignorance about him, they would both be very severely punished. Marjorie was determined

---

had everything packed in crates. These were eventually sent through the Red Cross to Sudetenland (Maffersdorf) where Ginzkey agreed to store them.

not to be browbeaten into submission of any kind, least of all an acceptance of the wretched accommodation they were providing for her and her children. Outraged, she demanded to see one superior after another but to no avail.

Marjorie's courage and tenacity coupled with her fluent German secured small concessions, but her persistent nuisance factor eventually bore fruit to some degree. Marjorie, Graham and James were moved from one camp to another, their longest stay being at Metz in Alsace.

The authorities finally tired of her and ordered her back to her husband's family in Sudetenland. Despite her protestations, they put the three of them on the train, under guard, bound for Reichenberg, from where she and the boys made their own way the three miles to Maffersdorf on the tram.

Of course, the family made them welcome but this too was a world away from Marjorie's comfortable life in the city. She had forgotten about village life. The contrast between Parisian apartment living and this *Kuh Dorf* [*One Horse Town in the Sticks*] could not have been greater. Being in Maffersdorf without her husband was an exile which threatened everything she aspired to and loved. The amenities in Anna and Josef's house were primitive. Water had to be fetched from a pump outside. The lavatory was not a flushing water closet and was housed in a wooden construction built on to the back entrance of the house.

When the weather permitted, Marjorie did the washing outdoors in a tub with a washboard, or *waschrumpel*. Clothes that needed boiling were heated in a large tin pot on the kitchen stove. There was mains electricity, but cooking was done on an old fashioned wood and coal fuelled kitchen stove which had to be lit every morning.

Reduced to these daily chores which had been assigned to others in those distant days in Paris, she often told Graham while scrubbing clothes at the washboard, 'I never thought life would come to this. I feel about a hundred years old.'

CHAPTER THIRTEEN

HITLER YOUTH AND GESTAPO THREATS

It wasn't just household chores that made their new life in Maffersdorf anything but easy. In a village of just 3000 inhabitants, they were watched constantly by the beady eye of the authorities. Graham found it extremely hard to have to lift his arm and say 'Heil Hitler' whenever he passed his teachers or officials in uniform. He and his friends decided to say it so quickly that they were just saying 'Heitler'. Sometimes they were caught out and had to repeat it properly but usually they got away with the trick, pleased with their small victory.

Most of the village inhabitants felt German, which indeed they were, both ethnically and by choice. Gustave's eldest brother Willi was awarded guardianship of Graham and James at the Gestapo's insistence, 'to ensure these boys are brought up as loyal German citizens.' Willi considered it his duty to interfere with Marjorie's way of bringing up her boys, even sending local lads to spy from outside their window to find out whether she listened to the BBC. Marjorie most certainly listened, but she knew it was extremely dangerous.

Then they received the tragic news that her closest ally, her brother in law Karli had passed away suddenly with a heart attack. Willi made life even more difficult but she had little choice but to shrug it off. During her second year in Maffersdorf, Marjorie was delighted when the Ginzkey family found her a little house in the village. She felt very fortunate to have her own place once more but the move, while affording her space from her in-laws, left her even more vulnerable to Willi's political attacks. Every Sunday, he would join a march past their house in full military regalia. Marjorie was in no doubt as to his disapproval of her.

She did make friends, however. One was a highly respected judge in Reichenberg, whose son fell in love with her and even proposed marriage, despite his knowledge of her situation. Marjorie remained loyal to Gustave, but she was not above using the friendship to secure the occasional favour where it became necessary.

One day, Marjorie received news from Gustave. He had hoped to find her and the boys still in France:

24.3.1941
Dear Heart,
I hope that you have received my latest news and confirm that I am now staying with Jean here. He sends you his best regards and thinks that it will be difficult for you to come and join me. I just don't know what kind of information you can get there but perhaps it is easier via Switzerland. You must find out the exact details on the spot. I had just hoped that I might find you here but now I must just continue to be patient. I am really so happy to know that you and our dear children are well, as well as all my dear ones at home. Do tell them all that they are very often in my thoughts. I have already written to Pierre for

clothes and underclothes and hope that he can send them to me.

I hope to hear from you my Dear soon, and to fold you in my arms and kiss our two dear boys and everyone at home fervently.

Write soon, Your Gustl

Gustave did not reveal that in fact his unit had been disbanded. He had to be very careful; he was now effectively a fugitive. However, Le Depot Commune des Regiments des Etrangers (the Legion) under Colonel Gaultiere had not left him entirely exposed.

He had been given a name to contact in the Vichy zone. Details were never written down for security reasons; they must be memorised. These were members of the Resistance who were willing to help returning Legionnaires with rehabilitation and temporary accommodation.

In the period after France surrendered, several groups had appeared. Frenay, who emerged as one of the leading Resistance chiefs, founded Combat in August 1940, and the liberal Catholic law professor Francois de Menthon founded the group Liberté in Lyon. It was there Gustave now found himself, with a poor family who gave him a room and did their very best to make him comfortable.

For the first five months from November to March he had lain low, working with and helped by the Resistance in Lyon. Gustave was never called upon to attack a den of collaborators or derail trains. He just tried to help out with simple surveillance tasks.

But lack of funds and his own self-respect forced him away from the reliance he was placing on others, who themselves were struggling to get by. A year in the North African desert with scant correspondence from Marjorie had left him with much to catch up on.

Jean, Gustave's old friend worked in the Lyon branch of the Societe Francaise Radio Electrique and was willing to put a word in for him. They had a vacancy for a job which he would easily be able to manage.

Jean very kindly offered him some accommodation and Gustave began his new role on 15th April 1941. Perhaps now life would regain a shadow of normality.

The details of Gustave's latest movements were conveyed to Marjorie through the Red Cross. She was unsure whether she felt relief, joy, or even envy that he should be back on French soil. She hated Maffersdorf. Newspapers told of heroic captures and the inevitability of the Reich's victory over Europe; Marjorie felt sure this was more propaganda than fact, and remained desperately concerned for Gustl's safety. She knew nothing of her family in England and wondered often how, and even whether, they were surviving.

She heard from Gustave again in May and June. He expressed concern about their apartment in Paris, exhorting her to make every effort to come and sort it out, apparently oblivious to the conditions they had suffered in the camp.

In the same letter, Gustave reflects how he would love to see his mother:

> 7-5-1941
> …The thing which would give me the greatest pleasure would be just to receive a few lines from my dear Mother. I hope she is well and that she has got over the pain over our poor Karli. I am sure that you my dear and our children are doing everything to make the end of her days as pleasant as possible…

In fact, Anna had passed away after a short illness during his absence in North Africa. Their first correspondence since his return to France had given Marjorie no heart to tell Gustave the sad news. They had always been so close; she knew he would be devastated, and he had already had to deal with the news of Karli's death.

While the war rumbled on, the boys were growing up. They attended the local village school and gained excellent command of the German language. However, they were treated badly by the local children. In school, they would call them *French Frogs* and *Luegenlords* [*Lying Lords*], a Nazi propaganda slogan. They would also say, 'You know we've got an English guy, an enemy among us in the classroom.' Graham and James frequently got into fights.

Early on during their stay in Maffersdorf, James ran into a barbed wire fence in the twilight and tore both arms just above the elbow so badly that the deep ragged wounds took a year or more to heal.

Graham became a teenager in the Spring of 1941, by which time he had already been enrolled into the Hitler Youth movement. At first Marjorie absolutely forbade it: 'Never forget, and always be proud: you are English. Hitler is our enemy', she said.

Before long, she had learnt that membership was compulsory for every boy over ten years of age. Any parents who refused to let their boys join would have them removed and placed into foster homes. Marjorie had no choice.

In contrast to his mother's horror at this development, Graham had, until now, felt resentful to be the odd one out. Having been chided by his peers, he was relieved to be able to join them now. He enjoyed the Hitler Youth meetings. They sang rousing songs that sounded good together and enjoyed sports and physical exercises which tested their strength and endurance. They all had to learn to swim and to ski in the winter.

The equipment was simple and primitive and the expectations high. The experience certainly toughened them up. 'The really dangerous part,' he later recalled, 'was the subtle indoctrination, which of course some of us were not mature enough to notice'.

The relentless pressure did not stop at school. The Gestapo made regular trips to the family home, persistent in their efforts to persuade Marjorie to disclose Gustave's whereabouts.

They saw her as an enemy in their midst, actively working against them. Marjorie became very frightened indeed when they threatened her and the boys' freedom, telling her that life in a concentration camp would be far worse than a transit camp. Memories of those awful days and nights moving from one camp to another came flooding back. What was she to do? She had no-one to ask. At her wits' end, she eventually went to her banker friend and his son for advice. They warned her not to carry this burden alone, telling her she must get word to her husband of the situation. She did just that.

A letter written by Gustave that December, with no address, is couched in much more guarded terms. He confines himself to hope for the future:

> …What more can I write except that I still hope that we shall meet again one of these days, that I think of you all the time. The only – and the best – Christmas present for me will be to receive a letter from you.
>
> Happy Christmas and with my best wishes for a good new year which will at last bring our sufferings to an end. I have received good news of your family who are all well.

A thousand tender thoughts and kisses for you and the children. My thoughts will be with you.
    Gustave

This news appeared to bear no trace of awareness of Marjorie's terrible fears for their own safety. She was in a frenzy of worry. How much longer could they hold off the Gestapo?

CHAPTER FOURTEEN

HINZERT CONCENTRATION CAMP

It was the end of January before Gustave received news that his wife and sons were being persecuted on his behalf. He immediately presented himself at the offices of the Red Cross and told them of his decision to surrender. He could see no alternative. They persuaded him that, in their opinion, he should have little to fear. It was explained to him which office to go to and what he should do.

In some ways it had been a relief. This way he could, at last, get word to Marjorie through a legitimate source without fear of consequences which might have to be borne by friends involved in their correspondence to date. His long-held dread of punishment being meted out to his loved ones was now becoming a reality.

Gustave's earlier relief was short-lived. When he walked into the offices of the Gestapo, his introduction was met with initial surprise. This act of surrender was not an everyday occurrence. Clearly bemused, the desk officer asked him to wait while he fetched one of his superiors. Gustave by now felt extremely nervous and uncomfortable. A Commandant appeared with a second officer and asked him to follow them into a room where he was questioned at length. They repeatedly asked him why he had not returned to Germany to fight for his country. He told them that when the war was declared he had been living in France for many years and was married to an English woman. When they found that he had been with the Foreign Legion for the duration of the war with France, they decided he must be interned, to 're-educate' him with German values and ideals. They saw no reason to explain this decision to Gustave, merely handcuffed him and took him into custody.

From that point he was allowed no outside contact. Gustave was desolate, lonely and powerless to contact his loved ones. The first they would hear of him would be notice of his incarceration. He dreaded the worry and pain that this would cause them.

To the Nazis, those selected for Hinzert were fortunate indeed. A number of the passengers on the train were captured PoWs, many of whom were legionnaires. Others, like Gustave, were not German born but were citizens of occupied territory. The overarching objective was to convert every one of them to an acceptance of Hitler's vision of the New Germany. Seen from the train, on which Gustave had been joined by a number of other prisoners and a couple of guards, SS Special Camp/Concentration Camp at Hinzert appeared idyllic. Its setting, in glorious countryside, belied the reality.

The apparent idyll was destroyed immediately on arrival. Gustave and his fellow captives went through the ritual of the *eingang*. On arrival they were met first by one guard who marched them into the camp in rows of three. They were then drilled into two rows in front of the *buro* where they were met by a very smart Lieutenant

Heinrich. Nicknamed Napoleon because he had a habit of sticking his fingers in his jacket, Heinrich was followed by a big beefy sergeant.

After Heinrich had walked down each row to inspect them, a so-called Report Fuhrer, responsible for the numbers in the camp, came out to meet the sergeant. He asked the prisoners in French to answer to their names, which were soon replaced by numbers.

'Shut your mouth, you!' he roared when somebody dared to speak. They were all frightened out of their wits.

All of a sudden six more SS appeared. Two positioned themselves on each side of the prisoners and two behind. They all held machine guns.

Commandant Egon Zill[9] returned with a big German Shepherd dog who sat obediently at his feet. Silence fell.

When the Commandant began to talk, he told the prisoners they were enemies of Germany. They were classified not as resistants, but terrorists.

'When you change your attitude about Germany we might let you out of here,' he told them in German.

The Report Fuhrer was translating into French and asked, 'Has anybody here not understood?'

When one boy put up his hand the Report Fuhrer threw himself through the ranks and punched him almost into insensibility.

They were then herded into public showers and each person was stripped naked by a fellow who used sheep shears to cut their hair. Blood ran all over their bodies which they were told to wash down with sackcloth dipped in neat disinfectant. Tufts of hair were left

---

[9] Egon Zill left as Head of Preventive Detention at Dachau to succeed Hermann Pister as Commandant on 19.1.42. See p.280

carelessly on their heads. The final indignity for the thoughtful and fastidious Gustave was the realisation that they had all become clones.

Amongst the French, the first sign of resistance came when they were asked to hand over their wedding rings. Their attempts at resistance were met with blows from pickaxe shafts. Gustave glanced around him in horror. People were falling all over the place.

By the time the new prisoners were naked and clean, liceless and hairless, clothes were thrown at them. Not the striped pyjama Gustave had half expected, but old army uniforms from the Czechoslovakian or Polish army. Some of them had been dyed black, but they all had a yellow stripe down the back of the coat and yellow stripes down the sides.

Once they were all kitted out, the men gave their numbers at second roll call; many received another kick to ensure they were in their place. They were allocated to billets, or huts.

On arriving in his billet, Gustave soon discovered that the prisoners had elected a leader amongst them. This man seemed to be able to haggle with the guards on their behalf. It was clear that the toughest and most brutal of the inmates, many with criminal backgrounds, seemed to rise to the surface in this new environment. This self-appointed power gained some degree of respect from the rest. Brute force seemed to evoke a rather grudging respect from the guards.

By the end of the day they were all desperate for food and looked forward with some relish to the promised evening meal in the canteen. They were greeted with a bowl of warm water purporting to be soup. Those who had preceded them in the queue had polished off whatever bread there was for accompaniment.

Later that night, lying on his bunk (such as it was), Gustave listened to the stifled sobs from the youngest of his group. Only fifteen years old, the lad had been allocated to the same hut. Gustl's heart sank. He knew that any move to comfort the boy would result in a beating for both of them.

His thoughts turned to his own eldest son. He had missed out on the first two years of Graham's life. This felt like a new sacrifice; it was now three years since they had been together. Graham was on the verge of manhood, his fourteenth birthday fast approaching, and without the guidance and love of his father. Gustave lay in the dark in despair.

'Would I have felt any different now had I not married my English rose?' he wondered. After all their efforts to be together and live in the country they both loved, there now seemed no hope at all for them. France was now part of the New Germany. Unless Britain and her allies could liberate them, there would be nothing left there for him and the family once this whole rotten business was over. Reflecting on his forty-one years, Gustl felt like an old man. He signed off one of his letters to Marjorie, 'Your faithful old Gustave'.

What the Commandant referred to as hard work came as a shock. All correspondence was vetted: Gustave's letters were written in perpetual fear of censorship and punishment.

Marjorie was greatly distressed when she received the next news from her husband. Addressed from *Durchgangslager* [Transit Camp] Niederbuhl[10], Stube10 and dated 19 February 1942, this latest letter was written in

---

[10] Niederbuhl: see Operation Pistol. See p.280

German, carefully worded in the knowledge that the Commandant would read it:

> ...Now if I had ever in my life been in prison and felt what it was like to be there when you know there is no forgiveness, you can well imagine how I felt...
>
> I have never seen so much snow and snow drifts in my life as in the last few days. Early yesterday we left this camp and arrived here yesterday evening, where it is very nice. This is a Work Camp. At the moment because of the cold and snow there is nothing to do. However as soon as it gets warmer we will go to work on the autobahn.
>
> The time spent waiting will now be much less difficult than it was before, now that I know that it is all just a formality and freedom really will bloom again once more. Our Camp Commander is very friendly and I hope that he will allow me to send you a telegram today in which I shall request you to send me 50 Marks from which only a small sum will be paid out each week, since none of us has a penny...I will also ask you to send me a little food parcel each week by express post, no luxury goods, basically bread and only when it is possible a little butter or another kind of spread (if possible in tins) and especially a little hard sausage and above all a couple of cigarettes which I miss most. Our Commander has in fact told us that we will get 3 a day but probably only in 10 days' time. I have only smoked perhaps 2 cigarettes in 14 days...About your coming here, I think, although I long to see you so much, that it is too early at present. We can in fact have visitors every first and third Sundays but I would still prefer if at all possible that you see me first when I am free...I believe that you agree with me and as long as we can at least write to each other, that is wonderful. I only regret that I did not put on the right clothes for the camp. If I had known, I would not have put my best brown winter coat and serge suit into the sample case and (instead) put on old things

and ski boots. But I will see, perhaps I can still send my good things home and you could send me something old...

Now dear child, don't worry about me, it will all work out in the end and then we shall be completely happy and try to forget all the sufferings we have endured for a few days. I beg you to hang on bravely and take care of your health. I too feel I am an old man and weigh only just 50 kilos. But we shall make up for it all. Once I am free, I will wire you so that we can meet in Berlin and spend a few days together there...I hope [the children] are well and in good form. Are they still in the children's home in R. and how do they like it there. Hug and kiss them for me. Gustl should write to me often, he is quite big enough now.

I will close now for today with my heartfelt greetings and kisses.

Your old Gustave who loves you.

Marjorie was in despair. It was she who had led him to this. What had she done? But had she really had any choice? The guilt was terrible. She made her decision. At all costs, whatever the risks to herself, she must find him and secure his release. She sent food immediately, some of which miraculously got through and he was able to share with his fellow inmates.

1-3-42

My Heart,

The day before yesterday I received your two parcels, one with the underclothes, which are very welcome and the other with the good things some of which I hope you are not doing without over there, if so you certainly mustn't send anything more. You surely won't have too much of anything. I was especially delighted by the letter from my boys and the fine music report...I hope that at least the Mallmanns will send the letter I requested to Berlin. I can already see that the only one thing left is to wait for my turn. I am in any case not included in the transport this week, but the Gestapo are coming here tomorrow and perhaps I will hear something. The next transport should be going to Kislau in two weeks. But we must not be impatient, as you say yourself…Of course I will telegraph you as soon as the happy moment arrives for me and then you can bring my good suit with you and we shall spend a few lovely days in Berlin. I can imagine that there are lots of things to be done there…Don't worry about my weight, it will soon increase with such fine parcels, our Commandant assured me yesterday. I feel very well at this weight and that is the main thing…

I am glad that the boys have been able to do plenty of skiing this winter. I have often thought of it in Hinzert. Isn't it amazing that when we so longed for snow for sport, it didn't come, and now there is such a long, hard winter, when we cannot use it.

And now, my dear, I will close again for today. Today is Visiting Day and there are certain to be many visitors. We had some here last Sunday but they had to leave early. I am already looking forward to your next letter and send you my heartfelt greetings and kisses.

Your Gustl.

The letters sent to Marjorie from the Niederbuhl camp increased her guilt and fear. Until now worried for his wellbeing, both physical and mental, she now understood that Gustave's life was in danger. The news that there were visiting days gave her the final impetus to plan the journey. She would track him down and fight for his release. The next letter reinforced her decision.

4-3-42

…I was called in yesterday for questioning here [after waiting several months] and am now much more confident that things will move quite quickly, perhaps even more quickly than we thought. If you have not already done so, you do not need to take any further action. I think it would be pointless and one must just allow things to take their course.

I am only angry with myself that I wrote to you about my weight and about parcels. Listen, dear child, you do not need to worry at all about these things, I am not as weak as that. You certainly should not send me everything you get, that would be crazy. The provision for us here is now quite sufficient and if you want now and again to include a few bread coupons which you can spare in a letter, that will be quite enough. You must however change your coupons which are not valid here for travel coupons.

Everything else is superfluous and, apart from the fact that it will not be fresh when it arrives, it will only be shared out here. There are perhaps two men in the whole hut who get parcels, and the others have nothing at all, and happy as I am to share with comrades, it would not be right if you were going without…Console yourself, my weight will soon increase quickly once I am home and can once again now and then eat schnitzel. From next Monday we will probably be working and then our provisions will be increased further…'

One letter appeared to suggest an interview with Konrad Henlein, with whom Gustave had a distant family connection. A Maffersdorf man and influential politician, Henlein had been one of the main agitators for German annexation of the Sudetenland[11], and now held the title of SS Gruppenfuhrer. As the party leader of the regional branch of the Nazi party he now governed Sudetenland. Marjorie certainly did not want to seek an interview with this dangerous Nazi; she assured herself

---

[11] Konrad Henlein, see Bibliography *Munich Agreement* p.277

that Gustave was name-dropping for the benefit of the censors.

Gustave himself was thankful that his letters, heavily censored, could not convey the squalor, the torture and the wretchedness of the living skeletons who had become his friends.

Self portrait of another inmate, Jean Daligault, March 1944
Source: Musée de la Résistance et de la Déportation (Museum of the Resistance and Deportation)

It was his weight loss, mentioned in an earlier letter, which frightened Marjorie the most. Despite his warnings not to do so, she determined to visit him there and do everything in her power to obtain a release for him on grounds of ill health.

Gustave had, in fact, lost nearly half his body weight, so he had mixed feelings about his wife's plans. He was filled with dread at the thought of her seeing him in this emaciated state, yet he still harboured hope for his release and urged her to try through official channels. At the same time, he yearned for the day when he would set eyes on her again. They were nearing their third year of separation and when they had last been together he had retained his fine looks. What would she think now of this shadow of a man?

At night after the hours of hard labour and food deprivation, he would try to recall the romance and passion of those early Paris days. Ever more difficult to recall, that was another world; here, he began to despair that normal life would ever be resumed.

The number of food parcels which arrived from home had to be shared out with his fellow inmates, so in fact did little to assuage his hunger. On the other hand, they did provide a huge uplift to his morale, as did the small supply of cigarettes which he craved.

By mid-March 1942 Marjorie's patience had run out. She had taken letter after letter to the town hall in Reichenberg to try to obtain their assistance in securing Gustave's release. Aware that her continued refusal to sign papers swearing allegiance to Hitler no doubt impeded progress, she nonetheless used all her intellect and as much feminine charm as she could muster in the circumstances.

Local contacts were a waste of time. Terrified that if she didn't succeed in liberating Gustave soon it might be too late, Marjorie completed her arrangements. She had already managed to find a small children's home; Graham felt far too grown up for this, but she gave him no choice. 'It is your duty to look after your brother while I go to bring Papa home.'

She had done a great deal of research and sought a lot of help from the Bischoffs, the wealthy bankers who had befriended her. Now it was time to act. Marjorie prayed that it would not become necessary to use her trump card: their connection, however distant, with Konrad

Henlein. Realising that this may well do more harm than good, she determined that was a risk simply not worth taking. 'Be good', she told Graham and James. 'I am going to find your Papa'.

Once she had left, Marjorie's heart constricted when she thought of her boys. Would they feel abandoned once more? She told herself firmly and repeatedly that there was no choice. The important thing was to keep everyone alive and safe. The boys would be looked after but their father's life was in critical danger. She must put her husband first.

Marjorie was gone for some weeks. Her journey took her more than 800 miles, from Reichenberg in the north east close to the Polish border right across to Niederbuhl, a small village near Baden Baden in South West Germany. She took with her letters from Herr Mallmann, his ex-boss, confirming that Gustave was Ginzkey's agent for France and that when the war broke out he had been domiciled in Paris for technical reasons. He advised Gustave was a member of DAF[12]. She also had with her a similar testimonial from Otto Bischoff. The originals of both documents had been sent, at Gustave's request, to NSDAP[13] Centre for Returning Soldiers, which he was convinced would also help to speed up the investigation of his case. She also took a letter from the old Ginzkey family doctor, explaining the family's medical history. His brother Karli having died in his early forties from a congenital heart condition, the

---

[12] DAF: The National Labour Front was the National Socialist trade union organisation
[13] NSDAP: Commonly known in England as the Nazi party

letter confirmed that Gustave's deteriorating health would not enable him to survive the conditions there.

Marjorie caught the train from Reichenberg and made several connections before reaching Rastaat, only a few kilometres from her final destination. At this stage her main emotion was excitement – to think that she would soon be reunited with her husband after so long a separation!

At the ticket office, she asked if there was a bus service to Niederbuhl and was grateful when a gentleman offered to give her a lift to the camp. Although her German was good, she was afraid that her English accent would deter people from talking to her, but this kind man was even able to suggest somebody who would put her up for a night or two. This was a miracle indeed, as she had set off with no idea of where she would stay. Her sole objective was to secure Gustave's release.

'Please take this telephone number,' said her driver. Having listened to her story, he couldn't help but admire her courage for making this trip alone. 'There should be a bus to coincide with visiting times but just in case, I don't mind coming back to fetch you. In the meantime, I will contact Frau Schmidt and ask her if she has a room for you'.

He dropped her at the camp. It was mid-afternoon and, uncertain of visiting times or days (Gustave's letter had only mentioned Sundays and this was a Friday), Marjorie took a chance on the reception she would receive. Perhaps they would just send her packing. On the other hand, perhaps they would be human after all. She said a silent prayer.

Standing alone at the gates, Marjorie's heart started to pound. She fought to quash the fear and eventually, the excitement at the prospect of seeing her Gustave resurfaced.

The guard at the entrance asked for her name. 'My name is Marjorie Lange and you are holding my husband Gustave Lange who should not be here. He is a German citizen! I am here not just as a visitor; I really must be allowed to see the Commandant.'

There were endless forms to complete; Marjorie's patience was tested to the limit when this exercise had to be repeated at several stages. At last she was given a visitor's pass. To her surprise she discovered that she would be permitted to visit Gustave that evening.

Eventually the moment arrived. She found herself in a large, empty waiting room. A guard appeared and escorted her into the hall, which was lined with SS almost outnumbering their charges. Marjorie scanned the room, her eyes alighting on a stranger behind a desk. The guard showed her to the empty chair facing him and ordered that they only speak in German.

When she looked into the man's sunken eyes, she barely recognised her husband. Marjorie was deeply shocked by what she saw. Her handsome man reduced to this! His forty-one years looked more like sixty.

'Meine liebste Marjorie,' said Gustave, tears rolling down his face. How desperately he wanted to embrace her but that was completely out of the question. She, too, was taken aback at the strict discipline imposed on them, but the most important thing for her was that she had finally found him.

Despite the close observation, the words and feelings which had been denied them for so long poured out. There was so much to catch up on with news of the boys and Gustave's family, that little of a sensitive nature was even considered in that first meeting. Time was up before they knew it but she promised faithfully that she would return. In the meantime, she determined, she would be working on her master plan.

Marjorie had little choice but to telephone her kind driver, who turned up as promised to collect her. He took her to the home of Frau Schmidt. Known to all the locals as the provider of bed and breakfast to those visiting loved ones at the camp, Frau Schmidt was warm and friendly towards Marjorie, who stayed with her for more than two weeks. She was able to give inside information, seeming to know more of life inside the camp than it was good for her to know, thought Marjorie, keeping her guard up. When she told her that Gustave had been transferred from Hinzert, Frau Schmidt explained that the previous year, two trucks had transported 70 Soviet PoWs to Hinzert. The prisoners were told they would undergo a medical examination, and mysteriously disappeared. Rumours abounded for months afterwards that they'd been injected with cyanide and were buried in the neighbouring forest[14].

Through her disturbing but revealing conversations with Frau Schmidt, Marjorie also discovered that the very month before Gustave's incarceration, the so-called Night and Fog directive was signed. Many NN (Nacht und Nebel)[15] prisoners transited through Hinzert on the way to larger concentration camps where they would eventually disappear.

She had to get Gustave out of this deadly place at any cost. In the first instance Marjorie demanded to see the officer in charge. This was met with a severe rebuttal. 'He

---

[14] Later borne out to be true [15] See Bibliography: p.277

does not hold interviews with wives of prisoners. Who do you think you are?'

This only strengthened her resolve. The Bischoffs had supplied her with plenty of Deutsch marks and Marjorie had learned many times throughout this war that even the enemy had their price. If the situation demanded, it had become commonplace when one was asked to provide ID to slip a note in with the document. It was remarkable how officials could suddenly speed up the process, or better still, produce results which would have been impossible without the extra incentive. 'Just think of it as a tip', a friend had once told her.

Back at Frau Schmidt's, Marjorie prepared her speech for the Commandant. She had the medical certificates to back her up and she would devise a very compelling story. She was quite prepared to lie about her commitment to the Führer so long as she did not have to sign up to it.

The next visiting day, she passed through the reception gate as she had the first time. When she reached the next check-in post she found it manned by a single guard. He was not a senior officer – probably just as well, she thought, he may not have the authority to grant her request but he was almost certain to know somebody who did. She passed her documents to him but this time she included a crisp large bank note. She managed to hide her nerves as she waited for his reaction. He looked at her quizzically but said nothing as he stamped her papers and returned them, slipping the note into his pocket.

'I need your help', she said. 'It is not a big thing. I simply must have the chance of an interview with the Commandant. I believe I have some information which will be of interest to him. Can you please arrange it for me?'

The guard shook his head but she was not going to give up easily.

'If you can give me good news when I come next visiting day, there will be more', she promised.

Marjorie was well aware of the risk she had taken in her approach to the junior officer. She could not completely trust her landlady either so when Frau Schmidt had reassured her that locally employed soldiers were open to bribes she had been very careful not to give too much of her plan away to her. Nevertheless, as money was always short and the custom was fairly commonplace, she convinced herself that such a move was unlikely to result in her own arrest. This was a risk was worth taking.

On the due day she arrived with much trepidation. As she approached the second check-in post, to her disappointment the familiar face was not there. Her heart sank and then raced with fear. She handed in her pass, first surreptitiously removing the note she had placed inside with such optimism. Gustave knew nothing of her secret so she must not let him see her disappointment. Although his letters had referred on more than one occasion to a meeting with the Commandant, there was no way this matter could be discussed during the visits because of the close scrutiny. They were both fearful that one wrong word picked up by the guards could delay his release – at worst, forever, given Frau Schmidt's stories.

That visit was an empty one indeed. Conversation centred only on the dates and times of her return to Maffersdorf. Gustave was worried about her absence from the boys and kept reassuring her that his case should surely be heard any day now. It had been wonderful to see her. 'We will soon be together in our own home. I know it. You really must prepare to return. I will be OK,' he insisted.

But how could she contemplate leaving him without having made any progress at all? It was so frustrating having to wait so long for the next visiting day. Marjorie prayed fervently that night for something good to happen in the meantime.

At the next visit, to her great relief the young guard was there to greet her at the second check-in. Impassive, he took her pass complete with banknote. Having wondered whether her trust would be repaid, she watched as he switched the money for a small envelope. She thanked him and moved on without showing any emotion, impatiently scanning for somewhere safe to tear it open. Today there seemed to be more guards than ever milling around. The lavatories were just off the waiting room! With pounding heart, she requested permission to go and retreated into the privacy of the cubicle.

The envelope was blank. The suspense remained until she finally pulled out the contents. Short and clear, the note read:

> 'An appointment has been made for the Commandant to meet Frau Lange at 3pm Wednesday 25th March 1942.'

Only three days away! Marjorie's prayers had been answered and she gave thanks silently. She was bursting to tell Gustave but dared not mention it during the visit. It would be dangerous to raise his hopes, let alone alert the guards who would certainly ask questions.

She rehearsed her speech late into the night for the next two evenings, debating whether she should appear assertive or demure. She dared not discuss the matter with Frau Schmidt. For the first time in her life Marjorie felt truly daunted.

She presented herself in good time on the allotted day and was not kept waiting. The Commandant shook her hand and immediately put her at her ease by showing her to a chair in front of his desk. As she spoke the carefully rehearsed words, her nerves steadied.

Somehow, her confident speech appeared to evoke his compassion. She finished her monologue with one short plea: 'Please release him!'

'It is not in my power to do that. This is a transit camp, it is under the jurisdiction of the Gestapo in Karlsruhe.'

'Surely you are the one who can recommend his release to the people in Karlsruhe?' she said. 'I will contact my influential friends unless you give me your word that my husband will be released'.

The Commandant first stared at her then walked over and looked out of the window. He had already received his own transfer papers and had been informed of the name of his successor, who would certainly show no leniency in a case like this. There was a long silence before he turned around.

'Frau Lange', he began, 'You have impressed me with your courage and I am to be leaving here in a matter of weeks. So I shall have to get moving on this. If you will give me your word that you will encourage your husband to be a good German citizen and will register with the authorities on his return to Reichenberg, I will pass on my recommendations to the Gestapo for his release. It will not happen overnight but it will happen. You must also promise me that nothing of this conversation will ever be repeated to any person outside this room.'

'You have my word, Herr Commandant, and I thank you most sincerely,' she vowed.

'We are not all Schweinhunds!' he added.

Marjorie felt triumphant and could hardly contain hr joy. She felt sure that the Commandant would keep his promise despite the difficulty she'd had in gaining an audience with him. Aware that men of all ages were by now being called to fight, Marjorie's only concern now was that this could require Gustave to take up arms on behalf of the German army. As she travelled the long journey home on the next available train, she prayed he would be spared this after all his sufferings.

The following weeks were agony. On April 18th 1942 a telegram arrived.

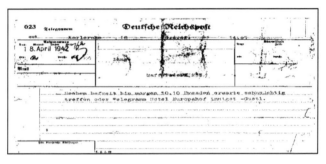

'Was freed this morning 10.10. Meet me Hotel Europa, Dresden...'

Marjorie took both of the boys by train with her, little James smart in a sailor suit. Graham was preoccupied with a small decorative fish tank in the hotel lobby.

The wait seemed endless. Their mother was on edge. Had something happened to delay his release? Then the revolving doors moved again and Marjorie ran into his arms. 'Gustl! Darling! At last!'

Holding Gustave at arm's length to study him, Marjorie was deeply shocked at his condition. She watched the same emotions flicker across her eldest son's face with a pang. The boys hadn't seen their father for more than three years, and the change was dramatic. Weighing just 48 kg, Gustave looked tiny and emaciated, his eyes sunk deeply in their sockets.

She watched Graham wrestle with the shock of realisation: had their Papa been in that camp much longer, they would never have seen him again. Marjorie pulled all three of them towards her in an attempt to expunge the thought. They were finally together once more; never again must they endure such a separation.

CHAPTER FIFTEEN

GLIDING INTO CONSCRIPTION

After a period of recuperation, to everyone's great relief Gustave was found unfit for the army, which at this stage in the war was conscripting men well beyond his age. He did, however, join the Home Guard. Never for one moment during those heady days in Paris did he imagine that he would be put to work on the floor of the Ginzkey factory.

Once the setting for Gustave's long and successful career, the factory had now been expropriated from the owners. A munitions manufacturing unit replaced some of the weaving looms.[16] Most of the workers were French forced labour or prisoners of war.

Gustave ignored the dangers of being seen to collaborate with the enemy, speaking French with the PoWs and forced labourers. He also smuggled them cigarettes and sometimes potatoes from the local farm outside working hours.

Gustave's sympathies with the PoWs did nothing to improve relations with his brother Willi, whom he had

---

[16] See p.281

already taken to task on more than one occasion since his return. Gustl knew that no-one, least of all his brother, could be trusted. He had to tread very carefully. With both parents and his favourite brother Karli gone, he had no one else to turn to other than his sister, who was powerless to help.

The family was together in Maffersdorf for nearly two years. Though life was hard, they came to accept their lot. Surrounded by lakes and mountains, the snowy winters enabled them to ski, while sunny summers went some way towards lifting their spirits.

During this fragile equilibrium, however, Graham and James were always being picked on and taunted. One day, ten-year-old James was confronted by a group of Hitler Youth on a narrow path leading up to the Main Street. He was alone. He tried to run away but they set upon him. Their 'wrestling' left him lying on the ground with his elbow shattered. For a while James couldn't move. His arm quickly swelled up a like a football. He walked home on his own with his entire arm swinging, unable to control it or move it in any way.

James was taken to Reichenberg hospital. The fractured elbow did not heal properly and the doctors prepared to amputate his arm. Only Marjorie's insistence prevented this happening. She took him to a hospital in Prague, where the elbow was re-broken and set again under ether anaesthetic. This time the arm healed adequately and an X-ray dated 23.XII.43 records the result.

By the second year of the family's reunion, the balance of the war began to shift. In early 1943 the Soviets completely cut off the German 6th army in the Battle of Stalingrad and continued to advance until they had won back the whole of the Crimea. This victory cost the lives of 140,000 German soldiers.

The Americans, who had been drawn into the Pacific theatre much earlier over the Japanese offensive on Pearl Harbour in December 1941, had finally sent ground troops to strengthen the European Alliance. By August 1943 when Mussolini surrendered to the Allies, the tide was turning sharply against Hitler.

One event had a particularly traumatic effect on Graham and James. Coming home from school one day they noticed a column of people, not walking but stumbling along the main road. The boys were heading downhill on a path converging with the road several hundred yards on.

As they came closer, they saw why the group did not move like soldiers. They were too weak, dragging themselves along. Some fell to the ground and lay there until guards with whips forced them onto their feet again. The people were dressed in grey prisoners' garb. The guards were women in uniform, SS women. Stunned, Graham and James both hurried on so as not to have to look. They ran home as fast as their legs would take them.

'What on earth has happened to you?' asked their mother. Graham struggled to articulate what he had just seen.

'They will be Jews being marched to their deaths,' she said.

'Why? What have they done?'

Marjorie explained that Hitler's final solution to his misguided 'Jewish problem' was their extermination. She told him about Auschwitz and other death camps, and that Hitler and Himmler, the Commander in Chief of the

SS, would not relent until the last Jew they could find was dead.

'Never get into a lorry. People are gassed while in transit' she urged the boys.

Graham was dogged by nightmares for years afterwards. Each time he was being hounded by the Gestapo and then being led to execution in various ways.

By now, Graham was studying at the Technical College in Reichenberg. His mother was praying that it would all be over before his sixteenth birthday when she feared he may be old enough for conscription. Just in case, she did her homework. Marjorie discovered that gliding qualified as pre-military training. In a vain effort to delay his call-up, in January 1944 Graham was enrolled in a gliding school in the hills of northern Bohemia.

Graham thoroughly enjoyed learning to fly. He did it the hard way, without a winch at first. They were simply catapulted by means of a heavy elastic rope which was stretched by twelve young men running and pulling it as far back as it would go. Then the instructor gave the order for the two or three who were holding the glider back to release it and off they went, learning gradually to lengthen the time in the air. That was the A test.

For the B test they were catapulted over a cliff and learned to fly, making neat turns without losing much altitude. To pass the test they had to make a right and a left turn and fly for more than three minutes.

Those three minutes were perfect bliss for Graham, being lifted by an upwind over the cliff and soaring gently to the whistling sound of the wind in the wires. He loved doing the elegant turns and then landing softly. He was looking forward to gaining the blue badge with three silver gliders on it to be awarded after passing the C test, when orders came for him to go straight to Prague. Military service could be delayed no further.

Graham returned from Gliding School to prepare and pack for his departure. Before his parents could tell him their news, it was clear from his mother's shape and size: she was expecting a baby in just a few months! Graham was overwhelmed by this news. His feelings were mixed at first. 'Surely,' he worried, 'after all they have been through, they are too old and tired for this. And with the future so uncertain...'

However, his parents' excitement was infectious. It took very little time for him to feel the same way and James, now eleven, was very happy about it. But Graham himself would be missing all the fun of this baby's arrival. Perhaps he would be allowed some home leave.

His parents were devastated by the news of Graham's call up. Marjorie dreaded it. Her son, still barely sixteen, would be so vulnerable. How could she face losing him? She had so nearly lost Gustave. What if he became a prisoner of war? There was also the ever present reality that he would be in conflict with her own brothers. She impressed on him never to forget that he was British. Relieved that she had returned to England for his birth all those years ago, she gave him a copy of his British birth certificate, urging him to keep it folded under the inner lining of his shoe. She also told him always to keep a pair of civilian trousers at the bottom of his rucksack:

'You never know when you might need them'.

Gustave echoed his wife's advice and hoped and prayed that his son's young life would be spared. The thought of Graham being subjected to the same experience he himself had had at Hinzert filled him with dread.

He told Graham to obey orders. Perhaps he would be lucky enough to fall into Allied hands. He had heard that treatment in Allied prison camps was fair. Marjorie and James said their farewells from the house. The family's time together had been so short-lived. They had filled this weekend with as much jollity as they could manage, although much time had been spent preparing and packing. There had been little time to dwell on the significance of the parting from their boy. Regardless of his age, from this moment on he was a grown man.

Father and son travelled together in silence to the station and caught the tram to Reichenberg. There, Gustave helped Graham stow his luggage onto the train for Prague. It was summer and the air was hot, especially in the jostle and clamour of the railway station. Both men felt cold and empty inside as they embraced. Graham, now much the taller of the two, felt a strange sense that he was also the stronger and desperately wanted to comfort his father. He would never have dared to articulate this.

'Please don't worry, Dad', he said. 'I promise you I will be OK'. After a prolonged embrace, Gustave fought to hold back the tears as Graham made his way to a seat. He cleared his throat and stood to attention, forcing a brave smile. Father and son waved to each other until the train passed out of sight.

CHAPTER SIXTEEN

ESCAPING DRESDEN – TO A BABY SISTER

Graham's gliding experience meant he was detailed to start as an Air Force Auxiliary in an anti-aircraft defence unit called FLAK.[17] Here he was to complete three weeks of basic military training. The regime was harsh but he and the rest of his intake got through it well, Graham relaying his enjoyment to his parents:

> 8/9/44
> Dear Mummy, Daddy and Jim,
> I'm waiting and waiting and there is still no telegram from you! The great event is taking a long time. And you even thought the baby would arrive early! When you leave me like this without any news, I get very impatient. How are you, Mummy? How lovely it will be when everything is happily over and we have a little screaming baby! I am

---

[17] An abbreviation of Fliegerabwehrkanonen, German for anti-aircraft guns. A flak corps was an anti-aircraft artillery formation employed by the Luftwaffe for anti-aircraft, anti-tank and fire support operations in World War II

already looking forward to it and to seeing you all again. How are you, Papa? There is certainly work again now.

Are you still having the same lovely swimming weather? The weather has changed here. It is raining and overcast the whole day. Everywhere you sink into the soggy mud. Thank God they have now made ash pathways. Just recently we've been on duty a lot, for example yesterday I was on duty from 7 o'clock to 1 pm and from 7 pm to 1 am. In the afternoon shift I carried out defence exercises as K1 on the altitude measuring machine and I also had to learn how to climb up the telegraph mast. It is all very interesting, but you just can't imagine how tired I am today. I am now one of the most important men on the gun emplacement not to have been called up yet.

Now I am going to bring the bread as there are two people in the bunker who have not finished their bread. The margarine we get is a kind of white mass, like cod-liver oil.

Earlier today I was not able to get on with my letter at all as we were already at our posts very early after one alert. Then at 11 o'clock there was another fire alert and the details of the [aircraft] positions that I could hear constantly coming in on the loudspeaker were extremely interesting. We were already set up to fire but yesterday there was a lot of excitement. We saw a couple of hundred Flying Fortresses flying around and they dropped bombs on 6-8 places. Then came a band of 24 Flying Fortresses directly towards us from a distance of 30 km. In a few seconds it was only 20km. Our radar had already shown activity.

Then the command came through: get ready to commence defensive firing at the direction of 11 o clock. The whole defence system swivelled into position and suddenly the bombers were gone again, towards Prague, and silver strips of radar-confusing aluminium foil were falling. Our Captain was already very excited but the boys even more so. There certainly wasn't one of them who wasn't thrilled. You should have seen it. When I am on duty next I must go through the aircraft position reports and records of flak firing kept in the writing station (hut).

Now once again I close this letter, hoping to be with you again soon.

Graham

The team was then sent to where the guns were positioned. Surrounded by earth walls, the guns were not normally visible. There, they learned to name the various parts of the guns and to handle the large searchlights, the lighter fast firing guns and, later, the 80mm cannons. Once training was over, they were divided into teams to man the searchlights and guns. They lived week after week in underground bunkers, although few bombers were sent to Prague because Bohemia, in the former Czechoslovakia, was then a Protectorate of Germany and there were very few strategic targets there.

They were very near Prague-Ruzyne Airport in case it should be attacked, but saw very few military planes. By now, Germany was already noticeably weakened, clearly not using the airport. The boys were relatively sheltered from the harshest realities of war, at least in the early days of their military lives.

4/9/44

Dear Auntie Franzi and Uncle Richard,

After such a long silence the villain writes once more. Aren't you still angry with me? As an excuse I can only say that the time between my visit to see you and the present has been so full of hurly burly that there really has been little time at home to think of and write to friends and relations. At last I have some peace!

I will now first ask how you are? Are you keeping well, and are you still so busy at work? At home, my sister has now probably already arrived! I would have loved to have been at home, but destiny had other plans!

Now I am sitting here in my *bivouac*, as I am the telephone operator, and can only think of home, and how Mummy must be feeling. At the beginning as I turned up on 3.8, we were ordered to Prague and I got to Rusyne (airport) with light flak and, when I finally finished my training after 4 weeks, I was again transferred here. I am near Prague, although I am not allowed to tell you where, it is at least nice that I can drive to Prague for outings. In Rusyne it was much nicer than it is here, although there is still a lot to learn about light flak. Here, with heavy flak, we have less defence instruction and fewer exercises but correspondingly more duty work and news-gathering. We also have school lessons for 2.5 hours a day, 3 days a week. If I weren't involved in procurement I would have little time to write. But thank God, I can send a few greetings to all the people I love. It was lovely when I was with you, and you were so kind, that I often recall the last beautiful days I spent with you before I was called up...I would love to be back with you again.

Now I'm afraid I must close as in 5 minutes I must hand over to the person taking over from me and then I must return to my group. So good-bye for now. I hope I will be able to come down and see you again. I would also be very glad to get a little message from you. Getting post out here is always exciting, we live in open fields where you can walk for an hour before you get to the next village, and letters are our only link.

With many good wishes,
Yours, Graham.

After six months Graham and most of his unit were transferred to the RAD *Reichsarbeitsdienst*[18] in Germany to be stationed in Radeberg near Dresden. This time they were put through even harsher basic training, including the use of the German army rifle, anti-tank weapons, machine guns and hand grenades. Even the food was much worse than in Prague.

On 14th February 1945, the Allies flattened the beautiful city of Dresden, completely destroying it. For ordinary Germans, this was incomprehensible. Unknown to the allies, the city was filled with refugees who had fled there from the East and West. Indeed, the bombing of Dresden by the British Royal Air Force and United States Army Air Force, remains one of the most controversial Allied actions of the Second World War[19] Just twelve weeks later, the German Armed Forces surrendered.

Shortly after the Dresden bombing, however, news leaked into their unit that the Allies were advancing fast on the Western and Eastern Fronts. The young soldiers knew the war could not last much longer. The German armies were fighting desperately against an enemy who now had massive support of men and material from the USA.

One day, Graham's unit received word that they were to be marched into Dresden to help defend it against the Russians invading from the East. This was shattering news. It would be suicide. A group of them did not sleep that night, discussing how they could escape. They slipped out of the barracks warily, only to see that

---

[18] *Reichsarbeitsdienst* Reich Labour Service

[19] In a recent study the 35,000 reported lives lost at Dresden has been reduced to 25,000. Whatever the number, devastation ensued. (See p.280)

floodlights covered the fence area. Soldiers patrolled the area with Alsatian dogs. They did not stand a chance.

The next day at 5am before dawn, they were called out and assembled on the parade ground.

'You are now going to have the privilege of playing your part for your country. Tens of thousands of heroes have given their lives in Russia under the most gruesome conditions. You are lucky in contrast to have the task of helping defend Dresden.

'Consider yourself upgraded from the RAD to the glorious German infantry. You will first build anti-tank defences and, when arms become available, you will be armed. I advise you to be men and to do your duty. Don't let the idea of surrendering or running over to the enemy enter your head! If you do not get a bullet from the front you will get one in the back. This company will be back here with packed kit in thirty minutes!'

The words sent a shiver down Graham's spine. 'If they get us into that city, we shall never get out alive,' he thought. He and a few of his unit decided they must somehow get away during the forthcoming two-hour march.

Opportunities did present themselves. The company was sighted and attacked by low flying aircraft. They scattered, pressing themselves into ditches or behind trees and edging away into the woods. But each time the accompanying officers were on the watch and counted them all back into line. They marched on.

As they reached the city they had to pass through an area where the road narrowed. Long tree trunks held by concrete supports, six feet high, closed the road to vehicles and tanks. Dresden had been declared a fortress, civilians evacuated.

'Why on earth should this ghost of a city still have to be defended?' Graham asked himself as he surveyed the ruins. Every house had been gutted by the bombing raid of February 14th; the entire town was destroyed by the firestorm caused by phosphorus bombs.

The men were weary and hungry. As they marched they reached a wide avenue. Suddenly the column stopped. Near the rear Graham saw two of the officers, who had walked fairly close behind them, cross the road to a group of army cars to ask a question. Here was his chance. At a point where a smaller road branched off at right angles not far behind them, he motioned to one of those comrades who had shared in the previous night's discussion. His friend hesitated, so Graham acted alone. He broke ranks and ran back around the corner, fully expecting a volley of bullets in his back. But no! All remained quiet. There wasn't a soul in that side street. Graham ran as fast as he could, jumping into the stairwell of a bombed ruin leading down into a cellar.

There he collapsed and lost consciousness. When daylight woke him, he knew he must find the courage to emerge back into the thoroughfare. He felt terribly hungry. He opened his backpack and found a piece of dry bread he had slipped in earlier.

His mother's advice now paid dividends. The civilian trousers were at the bottom of his knapsack. What a blessing! He changed into these, but had no choice but to keep on his heavy army boots. He left everything else behind, emerging cautiously onto the pavement. How would he get out of Dresden?

Graham decided to look for the railway station. On his way he looked up to see not one but many bodies of soldiers hanging from trees. All had boards round their necks reading, in German, 'I am a shameful coward. I am a swine'. They had been deserters; now, so was he.

Mercifully, he saw little activity. Military vehicles drove past but there was no one he could ask for help. Then, to his surprise he saw a lorry. He waved it down and it stopped.

'Where do you want to go?' asked the civilian driver, looking him up and down.

'Where to?' Graham replied. 'Out of town.'

The driver indicated for him to jump in and drove off. Not saying a word, he seemed intent on driving this truck as fast as it would go.

Suddenly they were confronted with an anti-tank barrier, with a narrow space on one side to let vehicles through. The driver was forced to slow down and a German soldier stepped out holding a stop sign. Graham was already working out what he would say or do if they asked him for papers or what he was doing. It was obvious he would be suspected a deserter. In panic he decided to try to behave as though he were mentally retarded.

He practised in his mind talking in a strange way, letting saliva drip from his mouth. But to his amazement, just as they were slowing to a stop, the driver put his foot down and made for the narrow opening. He nearly ran over the soldier, who fell and was too slow in getting up to stop them. They sped downhill and around a bend. Without a word, the driver drove at full speed until they reached some houses. There he let Graham out. With just a friendly gesture, he drove on.

Graham spotted a woman in a garden. 'Where does this road lead?' he asked.

'Bautzen', she replied. 'About 30 kilometres'.

'Where can I buy something to eat?'

She pointed the way to a little shop. Graham bought some bread and cheese, then started walking.

Making slow progress, he saw a bicycle leaning against a wall. No one was around. He got on it and cycled off. Some way along he met a group of German soldiers coming his way. They stopped him. Graham pretended he was one of the local lads. They only wanted the bicycle and he reluctantly gave it up.

He rounded a bend and suddenly, to his amazement, he saw the lorry that had given him a lift beside the front garden of a house. It was growing dark and he felt very tired, so he plucked up the courage to go into the house. Perhaps they would let him sleep there for the night. He reckoned that if the truck driver was there, they would not be Nazis who would give him up to the police.

His courage was rewarded. They shared their meal with him as he told them how much he wanted to get back to his parents near Reichenberg.

'Young man,' they said, 'You have a long way to go and you are heading in the wrong direction.'

It was a three storey house with other people living there. They gave him a mattress right up in the attic where no one would notice him. He was asleep in moments.

In the early hours of the morning he was awakened by someone shaking him.

'It's okay. You have nothing to fear,' said the man. 'Only we have thought about how you can best make it home. You don't seem to know that the Russians are already in Bautzen and it is not safe for you to fall into their hands.

'We think we have a better suggestion. I was in Dresden yesterday and saw that ordnance or hospital ships marked with large red crosses were docked by the quay near the bridge. Wounded soldiers are taken on board every day and are shipped up the river Elbe to military hospitals in Bohemia. Your best bet would be to get on to one of those boats as far as Leitmeritz and from there to get a train to Reichenberg.'

'You must be kidding!' retorted Graham. 'Nothing in the world will get me to return to Dresden. I am so glad that I managed to get out – by a miracle. No, never!'

'Well,' said the man, 'Think about it calmly. The Russians could easily take you prisoner and send you to Siberia. Goodness knows when you would be released. Even if you do not go east but try to go south through the villages, you will very likely fall into the hands of German or Russian troops.

'The safest escape I can see is on the Elbe, which takes you into Bohemia. I can give you a sketch which will help you get into the city through paths and back gardens so you do not have to pass that checkpoint. Of course, I can't promise that there will be Red Cross boats there this morning, but I am pretty sure there will be. There has been a regular service up to yesterday, and groups of wounded men keep coming.'

Graham paused. 'Thank you. I'll try it.'

Smiling, the man gave him detailed instructions. 'The journey will take you about three hours. Good luck.'

The man's wife, still in her nightdress, prepared him a hot cup of coffee and a bite to eat, and Graham set off in the dark.

Just past 5am, he felt optimistic as he passed the first landmarks the man had given him. Although it was pitch dark, he found the paths and went through the gardens, hoping no one would be up to see him. Gradually he realised he had reached the city. As dawn broke, he found the names of the streets he had to follow. Suddenly he was at the river.

Walking along the street which skirted the river towards a bridge, his mind raced. Would the Red Cross ships be there?

Yes, now he could see one, docked on the quay on the other side of the river, smoke coming from the funnel. He quickened his step. It was 07.55 on his watch.

Just as he was about to turn on to the big bridge, he noticed it had been closed to traffic and a few people were laying lines. Then the ship's horn blew. It was ready to leave.

'What shall I do?' he thought frantically. He decided to run across. A man shouted at him but he ran on. Then two others in front of him waved, pointed to the wires and shouted for him to go back. He hesitated but decided to carry on, not even contemplating that the bridge could be blown up whilst he was running. As he reached the end of the long bridge which stretched far beyond the edge of the river, he turned towards the boat. To his dismay it was moving slowly away up river. Graham slumped down onto a rock. Head in his hands, he fought back tears of anger and despair.

When he looked up again, he was surprised to see that the ship had not got very far; it was pushing upstream. He shook himself. 'What a fool I am. Why give up? Perhaps the boat will make another stop not too far away'.

He picked himself up. A passer-by told him, 'Yes, there is another stop,' and mentioned the name of a suburb. 'But,' she added, 'you know they won't take civilians.'

He ran up to the road and noticed a tram running in the direction he wanted, following the river. It was full of military personnel but he got on. Heavy boxes of ammunition were piled on the footplate where he stood. No one spoke to him. The tram caught up with the boat and passed it. His hopes began to return.

When they stopped, Graham watched anxiously as the boat caught up again while the soldiers unloaded all their boxes. The bus went on, passing several bridges, but they still seemed to be in the city. Then came a longer stretch, and another bridge. When he saw the landing place, he jumped out and ran across the road to find rolls of barbed wire which cordoned off the area where the embarkation took place. He noticed that someone had bent the wire before him. In desperation, he fought his way through it. His jacket was torn and his arm gashed.

A short line of wounded men was ready to embark. As he joined them, he exposed his bleeding arm, cradling it as if nursing a long held wound. He was taken on board without question.

What a relief it was for him to sit down among the men. They exchanged news of where they had come from. He told them he was from Radeberg and Bautzen where they had been confronted with Russian tanks.

At Pirna, the bridge over the Elbe was down so they had to change boats. Graham helped the wounded across. They continued the slow journey up river to Leitmeritz. Here, he disembarked with others who were taken to a field hospital nearby. Graham went to the railway station. It was late afternoon. He had three-quarters of an hour to wait for the next train to Reichenberg.

At the counter he asked for a ticket to Reichenberg. The ticket man looked at him critically over his glasses. Before he said any more, Graham saw a notice informing passengers that no-one was permitted to travel more than 50 kilometres.

'Where have you been,' said the official, 'if you don't know of this restriction?' He regarded Graham suspiciously. Graham thought it best to disappear.

Later, he found a young lady and asked her to buy a ticket for him to any place en route within the permitted limit. She understood and was willing to help. With that ticket he got onto the train and found himself in a carriage full of *Nachrichtenhelferinnen* [the Women's Auxiliary Signal Service]. Graham was relieved; he felt sure they too would help him. He was right. The women were willing to hide him from the ticket inspector, suggesting he crawl under the wooden seat. When the inspector arrived they had crossed the 50 km limit but he did not check them carefully – their military tickets entitled them to unlimited travel.

In Reichenberg Graham was only 5 kilometres from home. He changed platforms and waited for the next train in the direction of Gablonz. It was well past midnight and he still had to wait quite a while for the train which would take him to Maffersdorf, where he would at last be reunited with his parents and meet his baby sister, who must now be six months old. Graham's excitement was mounting every minute, but there were still one or two obstacles to overcome. How was he to avoid the guard when boarding the train, then get past the ticket collector when disembarking in Maffersdorf?

When the train pulled up, he watched the guard carefully. He walked right to the end of the train and jumped on when the guard was not looking. There were so few passengers getting on the train, Graham hoped the guard would be tired and sit down somewhere, but he took no chances. He stood on the rear platform outside the carriage. There were only two stops and he knew the train came into the station very slowly. He jumped off just before it actually reached the station and was able to run down a bank on to the road without being noticed.

It was only a fifteen-minute walk home. Now 2am, the sound of his boots on the road rang loud in his ears as he walked briskly to the house. Every sound seemed magnified by anticipation as he arrived in pitch darkness. He fumbled to find a box or something to climb onto in order to reach up and knock on the bedroom window.

Graham's heart was pounding. It seemed to take an age for a light to appear, then at last his father's face was at the window. Gustave opened it slightly and whispered, 'Who is there?'

'Daddy, it's Graham. It's me!' He ran to the door.

'I can't believe it!' cried Gustave, closing the door and throwing his arms around him. 'I can't believe it! Our boy is back, safe and well! Marjorie, Graham is here!'

They turned into the bedroom to find his mother in bed with the baby in her arms. Graham knelt down beside her, overjoyed, and buried his head in her side. He looked at his sister and kissed them both.

'Oh, I cannot tell you how happy I am! You can't imagine what I have been through. It's a miracle I am here. I can't believe it yet. Am I just dreaming?'

His heart still pounded. Had he really escaped what seemed like certain death? 'To find all three of you here, all well, and the baby, what a beautiful baby, oh, it's too much, it's overwhelming!'

Graham rested his head on the bedcover and the baby closed a tiny fist around his hand. Reaching out to embrace him, Marjorie's tearful gaze met her husband's over the heads of her eldest and youngest children.

Little James slept on safely in his bed. Now, at last, they were all together. She closed her eyes and sent up a fervent, silent prayer of thanks.

CHAPTER SEVENTEEN

SAVED FROM EXECUTION BY A PoW

The happiness of that homecoming had to be short-lived. Germany had not yet surrendered; Gustave and Marjorie agonised over what to do. They both felt it was too dangerous for Graham to stay with them, yet to send him away at such a time seemed unbearable.

Marjorie was desperate to keep her little family together but once more, keeping everyone safe must be the priority. She knew that so many mothers did not have this choice to make; they would never again see their sons. She tried to keep her tears to the rare moments she was alone, telling herself *you must be strong*. Gustave, too, wanted nothing more than to keep the boy at his side, but they reluctantly agreed: they would never forgive themselves if their own feelings put Graham in more danger.

Hitler continued to preach, 'We will fight to the last man. If we go down, we shall go down fighting as a German nation that is proud and we will die with honour. We will never again submit to the disgrace of capitulation.'

Women and older men who remained were being trained in resistance and to inflict losses on the advancing troops. After much debate, Gustave asked a Czech friend, Premysl Zantovsky to hide Graham until the war was over. A committed Communist and part of the growing Czech resistance movement, Zantovsky was a close and trusted friend. They had decided that he was their best hope that their boy remained safe.

Under cover of darkness Gustave took his son over the hills into the Bohemian Protectorate and left him there with a family he knew to be friendly. Communication was difficult; Graham could not speak Czech and the family did not speak German, but he quickly learnt enough to make himself understood.

Several weeks went by with no chance to see his family, but he was well protected and the war trundled on. Then on 30th April 1945, James's twelfth birthday, Hitler took his own life. Early attempts to cover up his suicide delayed the announcement until late evening on 1st May. Then a few days later after more than 24 hours of repeated broadcast appeals for Allied aid, partisans who had risen in Prague radioed: 'Help has come.' [20]

Confusion was spreading among the German troops inside Prague. Some were surrendering and were being disarmed. Some were fighting. Others were staying in barracks. All units were ordered to cease fire and await further orders.

By 3am one night three announcers, one speaking with an American accent, one with an English accent and the third speaking Russian, were all calling for help.

The day came at long last on 11th May, 1945 when Czech radio announced the news of Germany's

---

[20] Daily Telegraph report: Britain at War, London, May 1945 (p.280)

unconditional surrender. Gustave and Marjorie could hardly believe it and were cautious at first to celebrate. Certainly, everyone welcomed an end to this terrible war but to be on the losing side after all the loss of life, and in particular the devastation of Dresden: there would be mixed feelings in the village.

However, the general feeling was great relief; soon the village church bells were ringing with all their might, and then the sirens sounded. At last this terrible war was over. Graham lost no time in finding his way back home and the family rejoiced. Reunited, they celebrated their good fortune in having survived the war.

Their joy was short-lived. It turned out that the family's early caution had been justified. Within weeks the Russians arrived to take revenge on the Sudetens who, happy to be Germans, had welcomed Hitler in 1938 and appeared content to lose their Czechoslovak identity. Russian troops arrived, not in trucks or marching in columns, but in carts drawn by bullocks. Soldiers on foot stopped every person they could and demanded watches, gold rings and anything that took their fancy. On one occasion, planes flew overhead and suddenly a blast rent the air. People scattered in terror. A few bombs were dropped. One hit the church and damaged it severely. People ran into their cellars fearing that more would follow, but peace returned.

The whole family was at home when Russian soldiers banged on their locked door. Gustave had managed to find a French flag. As he opened the door, he spoke French then tried English, but to no avail. He pointed to their epaulettes and asked, 'Officer? Officer?' Receiving no response, he gesticulated his wish to go with them to find an officer. They kept saying 'Vodka! Schnapps!' and made signs that they should be given some. Gustave took them down to the cellar which contained only a heap of empty bottles and a cask of cider. Annoyed, they went back up and wanted to enter the rooms. Gustave again took them by the arm. Repeating 'Officer! Officer!' he persuaded them out. Graham followed. They led him to an officer who was standing beside a military vehicle. Again Gustave asked, 'Do you speak English? French?'

'No!' The officer shook his head and reeled off something in Russian. He ordered father and son to get in the jeep and drove them to another officer who understood some German.

Gustave tried to explain that he was anti-Nazi, had been in a concentration camp and that they had lived in Paris before the war; also that Marjorie and Graham were British by birth. Finally, his persistence paid off. The officer believed them and said he would instruct a soldier to guard their house. Once he was sure he had won him over, Gustave asked why they had bombed the village church when the war ended five days ago – Russian soldiers themselves could have been killed.

'They are boys!' laughed the officer. 'Before they have to stop, they wanted to have some fun. It did not happen on a Sunday so they guessed no one would be in the church. And Mother Russia has many children and one or two more dead – what is that when millions have been killed at the front?'

Father and son shook their heads and he laughed again.

When they arrived back home a number of aunts and nieces had arrived to seek protection. Stories abounded that these soldiers were raping women and girls, sometimes in front of their husbands and parents.

While the Russians were around, Gustave rarely left the house. So concerned was he that he called Graham into his room for a serious talk.

'I'm going to send you on an important mission. You are seventeen now. We must get out of here as quickly as we can, but I cannot leave your mother and the baby here just with you two boys. I will talk to the French PoWs and ask them to take you back to Paris with them. They are expecting to be repatriated any day now. Are you ready to do this? When you get to Paris you must go to our friends, the Sansons. I am sure Pierre will go with you to obtain the necessary papers for us to get our visas to return to France and join you in Paris.'

Graham welcomed the opportunity. The very next day they received a message from the PoWs that they were to be at a certain meeting place in Reichenberg at 8am the next morning where a convoy of trucks would take them to Gera, an assembly point in Germany. They began their preparations straight away.

Graham had no rucksack except a military backpack which a German soldier had left. Worse, he had no trousers which looked as though they would survive the journey. The only thing he could find was a pair of black riding breeches and riding boots, which he wore with a white shirt and a jersey.

Marjorie was not happy about the riding breeches as they looked like SS Officers' garb, but they were at least strong and warm.

She wrote a letter: *To whom it may concern*, stating that the holder was a British born subject, making his way back to Paris where they had lived as a family since 1930, in order to get the necessary papers to entitle the family to return to Paris. She stated that Graham's father had been held in a concentration camp for his anti-fascist stance and requested that every assistance be given to her son.

Early next morning and holding back tears, Graham bade farewell to his family once more. He walked the three miles over the hill to Reichenberg, but at the top, fighter planes suddenly swooped very low. They turned directly towards him and opened fire. He dropped into the little ditch beside the path and pressed himself hard into the soft damp soil, evoking memories of Dresden. He heard the bullets hit stones very near him. As fast as they came, the planes were gone. Graham sighed with relief, got up and continued on to the meeting point.

The place was teeming with PoWs. A sergeant was sitting at a table, carefully taking down names and checking any paperwork they had.

Graham noticed there were two officers in charge, a British one and an American major. He decided he would see the British officer. Graham showed him his mother's letter and his tattered and dirty birth certificate. After a few questions he said, 'No, I am sorry, you are not a prisoner of war. I cannot take the responsibility of taking you.'

Furious, Graham left him, but didn't give up. He decided to repeat the same exercise with the US Major, who responded to him in French. When Graham answered him fluently, the Major quizzed him as to why the family was in German territory.

Graham told him their story as briefly as he could. He stressed that the PoWs from Maffersdorf would vouch for his family, which they did. The Major looked at him.

'OK, jump into my jeep and stay with me. I'll see what I can do for you in Gera.'

They set off as part of a string of US military trucks full of men. In many of the places they drove through, people were gathered along the roadsides to watch. The US drivers and mates had fun throwing cigarettes out of the truck windows and watching locals scramble to get one or two.

The RAMP [Recovered Allied Military Personnel] Evacuation Centre in Gera was vast. For the first time he could remember, Graham had food piled so high on his plate that he could eat no more.

In the evening the Major, still keeping an eye on Graham, took him to a show where the Andrews Sisters were top of the bill. He had never heard that type of music; to him the harmony sounded very strange.

In her letter Marjorie had mentioned that her son might be useful as 'he speaks three languages fluently.' Here, they were short of English-French translators so Graham was asked to help out.

After a week or so, it dawned on him that his PoW friends from Maffersdorf had disappeared. He realised that, for his parents' sake, he should move on.

The American Major was understanding and made arrangements for Graham to leave on a train bound for Paris in two days' time. He ordered a Lieutenant to certify that he had checked his identity and issued permission for him to return to France where friends, whose name and address were stated in the letter, would receive him and assist in getting the necessary papers for his parents to follow.

To whom it may concern:

This is to certify that the undersigned has checked the status of the bearer (GRAHAM LANGE) and is satisfied that he is an English citizen and that his former home was in Paris France.

The bearer will contact and live with M. PIERRE SANSON, 4 Rue de Plaisance, Creteil, Paris, France who is a trusted family friend and adviser and who will assist in the repatriation of the bearer's parents from Liberec, Reichenberg, Czechoslovakia

*Any assistance that can be given to Graham Lange will be appreciated.
Signed T. W. Guptill,*
1ʳˢᵗ Lt.AGD
U.S Army,
SHAEF PWX Officer.

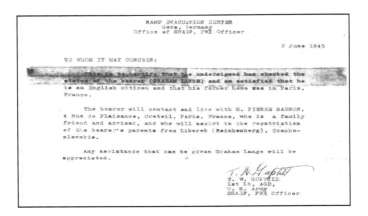

The Americans stuffed as many cans of food into his rucksack as they could before waving him goodbye.

The train was like a goods train with only one passenger compartment. All but the officers and some civilians were transported in cattle wagons. The railway line had been set up for emergency use and had to stop innumerable times. They made very slow progress, held up for hours or even a whole night in some stations because of construction work. By the third day Graham understood why he had been given so many cans of food; there was so little to eat and drink and even less chance to wash. They began to relax at the stops, jumping out and lying down to get a little sleep, until they were awakened by the train's whistle telling them to get back quickly. Inevitably a few got left behind.

Day after day the journey became more tedious. One day they stopped in open wooded country and went through the usual procedure. In a moment they were stretched out on the grass. After some time the whistle blew and they scrambled back into their cattle wagons.

As Graham climbed on board, he noticed two men in civilian clothes looking through his rucksack. One of them stood reading some letters. Suddenly he realised they were reading the letters which cousin Liesl had asked him to post to her fiancé in Germany.

'Are you the owner of this military backpack?' they asked.

'Yes, I am.'

They were clearly suspicious, especially because of his clothes and boots. They showed him their card and identified themselves as agents of the Deuxième Bureau, the French Secret Service. They searched him thoroughly but all they found was some German money.

'We have received reports from some PoWs who suspect you are German. Judging from your German accent, your army rucksack and the uniform, they think it likely you are an SS man. We have found letters in your rucksack which confirm that suspicion because they are written in German and describe the behaviour of the Russian occupation troops in Reichenberg in very derogatory terms.'

Graham was handcuffed and marched off towards the passenger carriage, where the officers were. They reported their find. Making much of the evidence, there was talk of an immediate verdict and 'execution'. They spoke in French, so Graham understood everything they said. Graham was terrified and pleaded with the officers to hear his story. He showed them the letters both from the US Lieutenant and from his mother. They debated what they should do. They asked his age and whether he had a birth certificate. He gave them his tattered and barely legible British birth certificate which he'd kept in his boots all the time he was in the German military.

Then Graham had an idea. 'I started out with a whole group of PoWs who had been in Maffersdorf,' he said. 'My parents had often given them food and cigarettes at great risk to themselves. When we arrived in Gera I stayed for a few days helping out as an interpreter and I think they must have taken earlier trains. But it could just be that there is someone on this train who could tell you all about my family and vouch for the truth of what I am telling you.'

The officers were prepared to explore this. They instructed the two Secret Service men to go through the entire train with Graham to see if anyone could identify him and confirm his story. They asked the men in the wagon they were in first. There was no-one. When the train stopped the officers got out and ordered everyone in the next wagon to stay in it while they asked them the same question. Again there was no-one. They moved to the next and the next and the next, with the same answer. Graham's heart sank as they approached the end of the train. They got into the final wagon, which was crowded. His heart was in his mouth as they asked and waited. Miraculously, a voice shouted in French, 'Mais oui! C'est Graham Lange!'

A man came forward called Pommier. He looked at Graham carefully and said he was in no doubt that he was the son of Gustave Lange. He had been very fond of Gustave, he said, because, 'although it was forbidden, he used to speak to us in French and he often supplied us with potatoes and spaghetti.' He told them of the victory celebrations to which Gustave's family had all been invited.

Pommier was taken to the officers at the front. They listened and asked questions, but were satisfied with his testimony. Graham was ordered to collect his German backpack and to travel with the officers for the rest of the journey.

Even after all this, Graham did not make it to Paris. In Lille he passed out from fatigue and doubtless delayed shock. They deposited him at the station. When he came around, Graham was in hospital and was given something to revive him.

'Where is my rucksack?' he asked anxiously.

'You were brought in just as you are,' came the reply.

To his despair, everything including a wallet with his small amount of money was gone. Fortunately, the important documents were still on him.

The following day Graham was discharged and sent on an ordinary passenger train to Paris, where he was collected by a representative from SHAEF, the French Repatriation Service. This man took him to a medical centre where he was examined, given a shower, had his clothes disinfected and his hair searched for lice. Finally, he was given some French money and released.

Although he was still not well, Graham was elated that he had made it to Paris. The money enabled him to take the bus to the suburb of Creteil, where he found the Sansons' house.

Astonished to see him, the Sansons welcomed him with open arms. He explained that he'd just been discharged from hospital in Lille. They gave him something to eat and sent him straight to bed, where he slept from the afternoon through to the next morning. After breakfast, the questions tumbled out. Pierre and Maria were horrified to learn of the ordeals their closest friends had endured during those years of war.

CHAPTER EIGHTEEN

FOLLOWING GRAHAM TO PARIS

Letters from his old friend Pierre Sanson confirmed to Gustave that he was trying to help Graham with the authorities. Pierre was the *fixer*. He had set up a little business roasting, packing and selling coffee beans. With his coffee he was able to barter all kinds of things which were impossible to buy on the open market. They tried hard to obtain Gustave's French citizenship but were told, 'It will take some time'. Moving from one office to another, they eventually succeeded in obtaining visas which were duly wired to the French Embassy in Prague, and eagerly collected. These would finally enable Gustave, Marjorie and the baby to return to France.

Throughout Graham's journey, much had happened at home. The second Republic of Czechoslovakia had been created. The new government wasted no time in punishing ethnic Germans for their collaboration with Nazi Germany for the secession of the Sudetenland from their mother country. Gustave received word through his Czech Resistance contacts that Uncle Willi and his family were on the list. Gustave too would have been, but for his well-documented anti-fascist stance. He went straight to his brother.

'Something is afoot,' he told Willi. 'I don't know any details, but if you have any valuables, trust me to keep them safe for you.'

They did so without hesitation. Gustave later found out that within days of his visit, Willi and his family received another knock on their door. A group of armed military ordered them at gunpoint to leave their home with one small case to each person. The family were stripped of any watches and jewellery they were wearing, then delivered to the railway station in Reichenberg. They were deposited on a westbound train to a destination unknown to them.[21] Their house, together with the house Josef had built and for which he had worked and saved his entire life, went into State control.

The new regime had enabled Gustave to obtain a Czech passport. Until then he had been deemed stateless. He was delighted to be able to travel again. In a timely coincidence, he was contacted by the owners of I. Ginzkey; they had been given back the rights to their factory. The owners wanted Gustave to return as a main board director as soon as the factory was refurbished with looms and spinning machines. His history with the company gave him the ideal qualifications under the new political regime. But Gustave's heart was in Paris. For Marjorie's sake and the family's, he felt he must return to France. He hoped that eventually they could reinstate him there, but it was far too soon for that.

---

[21] It is estimated that 1.6 million ethnic Germans were deported to the American zone of what would become West Germany. Several thousand before them died violently during a period of wild expulsions between May and August 1945 (see Expulsions: p.280)

Ginzkey wished him well and told him the company would always have a place for him. He even provided Gustave with large wooden crates in which to pack all their possessions; these were stored with the furniture in the factory.

On 18th June 1945 Gustave and Marjorie, along with James and his small sister, were repatriated to France in a Dakota plane with about 30 other people. They were reunited with Graham and the Sansons. As soon as the front door opened, they were greeted with laughter, tears and the aroma of freshly ground coffee. It was a great joy to be together again. They were delighted to be back in their beloved Paris and relieved to have escaped unscathed by the Russians.

The French Ministry for Prisoners, Deportees and Refugees which had taken over the prestigious Hotel Lutetia in Paris issued each family member with a *Carte de Rapatrié*. [Appendix J p.276]

Once more, their joy was to be short-lived as they struggled to find somewhere to live. They were each entitled to a cash sum, in James's case 5,000 francs[22]. The Mairie at Creteil gave them ration books, free Metro tickets and, where appropriate, tobacco vouchers.

At first Gustave, Marjorie and the baby stayed some distance from Creteil with Mr Vasseur, the headmaster of Graham's former primary school in Puteaux. James was lodged in central Paris, near the Gare du Nord, at the Institution Chaignon, 16 rue des Poissoniers in the 18th Arrondissement.

Later, with what little money they had, the family found a small apartment in Suresnes. They moved into

---

[22] 1945 rate was 480 francs to the £5,000 francs would equate to about £10 – c.£410 in 2018 value

empty rooms which they could not afford to furnish; it would take time before their own things could be shipped from Maffersdorf. Nevertheless, they quickly made friends with the neighbours. One piece of furniture after another was contributed, and gradually the apartment became a little home.

On their arrival in Paris, Marjorie's first thought had been to obtain a British passport for Graham. 'You were born in England, you have a right to British nationality,' she told him. At the first opportunity she took him to the British Embassy. The passport was issued without any difficulty. Graham was the only member of the entire family to own a UK passport; the document meant a great deal to all of them.

'You treasure this!' his mother stressed. 'This is the most valuable thing that you have, and that we all have, because all our hopes are fixed on you.'

She hoped she would soon be able to renew her own British passport; this way they could gradually obtain citizenship rights. Their prospects appeared very bad in France.

Gustave had a Czech passport but Czechoslovakia was now in the Russian Zone. Within months of the end of the war, Czech names had replaced German ones in towns and villages and the official language was Czech. German was no longer spoken. Gustave, Austrian at the time of his birth in 1900, had rejected German nationality. His claim for French nationality, promised in return for fighting in the French Foreign Legion, was likely to take up to a year to be cleared.

Marjorie began to get in touch with her pre-war friends. She found Lisa Steinhardt and her daughter on the third floor at 90 Chemin de la Fouilleuse, Cité Jardin,

Suresnes. Their apartment overlooked the green spaces towards the racecourse on the western outskirts of Paris.

Lisa and her husband Richard had been Marjorie and Gustave's bridge partners in the old days. Richard, a Jewish man, had had the foresight to leave for South Africa at the outbreak of war. He had left Lisa with a promise that he would send for her as soon as he possibly could. They had no idea then that their separation would be so long, much longer even than Marjorie and Gustave's. Lisa was desperate to join him; her enthusiasm for South Africa rubbed off on Marjorie.

Meeting once more, the two mothers recognised in each other the strain of those war-torn years. Their faces were now lined with the poverty, hardship, constant fear and longing for their loved ones. It was a great joy for them to meet again, spending many hours sharing their experiences while Lisa's seven-year old daughter, Eva, was the focus of much attention. But Marjorie could not ignore the questions which had been niggling away at her. Why was Lisa still here? What was stopping her from joining Richard? Surely it was safe for her to leave Paris now. Had she felt that he'd deserted her? It was not an unreasonable conjecture, after all – poor Lisa had certainly struggled to bring up her daughter single handed.

Perhaps the long absence had dulled her love for him. Or was she afraid of a future unknown? Marjorie was wrong on all counts. Lisa was simply not confident in the administrative nightmare (as she saw it) of acquiring the necessary visa documentation. Her passport had long since expired, and in any case she had to get Eva included in a new passport. She had been overwhelmed by the prospect of photos and form filling and all the rest of it.

'I am just a seamstress, not a secretary!' she explained.

For Lisa, Marjorie's return could not have been timelier. As a frequent visitor to the Immigration Offices, she was glad to help her friend with the visa and passport formalities. They speculated together about the new life in South Africa which beckoned and the excitement was infectious. She drafted this letter to Richard on the backs of four 'Controle Sanitaire des Repatrie' notices, and on three old order forms from I. Ginzkey, Maffersdorf:

> Dear Mr Richard,
> By the telegram from Lisa on the 19th you will have heard that we have arrived back in France after nearly five years of misery in Germany. It would take me far too long a time to tell you by letter the recital of our misadventures. Let it be sufficient that I tell you the chief occurrences, and that we are now at least out of the Hell and that during this awful time we very often spoke and thought of both of you, knowing our little Lisa alone in a Europe where a word could cost a head, thinking too of you, the only one among our friends who really saw the whole thing as it really was and would be, who prophesied the entire calamity foreseeing the result.
> How terribly naive I was. I was always very socially inclined. I must avow that although I loved our little dinners and afterwards our interesting political controversies to Mocca and liqueurs, I was definitely against your theories. I thought that I too, knew, that I was after all as travelled and well read as Mr Richard, but, having the softness of heart of a woman, that I understood better the necessity of a great change in the Government of Europe. I saw that there was misery and womanlike thought it could be altered.
> I have paid bitterly, bitterly for my naiveté. Now I know what you knew then, but to acquire this knowledge (of the German race at their worst) it was necessary to go through Hell and I would rather be without it for to have seen

humans descend to worse than beasts during years is almost too much for a sensitive brain. One feels one hundred years old.

You know that at the outbreak of war Gustave immediately volunteered in the French army, and left for Afrika in November. I remained in Paris with the boys. Until May life went on without a great change but then as the Germans began their offensive France went panic stricken and Paris especially – and then the Germans came – occupied our blocks of flats which were entirely empty except (for 2 families) we and another family opposite and it took them no longer than six weeks to discover that I was English and I was given the choice of concentration camp or – Germany, reminding me of course if they caught Gustave they would shoot him at once.

I chose naturally the latter hoping that in Maffersdorf I could do at least something for Gustl.

I was nearly three years there surveyed of course from the Gestapo. When this famous Institute discovered that through a friend in Switzerland I was hearing from Daddy I was forced always with the charming threat of concentration camp to do everything to get him back and after six months he came. At Saarbrucken they then put him instead of me straight in concentration camp. With a thousand difficulties he eventually was released and took his work at Ginzkey's up again.

(Now of course) The war has ended, the nightmare has taken an end. With Gustl's French military papers as proof that we could not be more active against the Nazi regime, we were given marvellous papers by the Czechs. Gustave was asked to take over the factory but the French Delegation in Liberec, having assured us of our right to repatriation to France and having suffered so much longing to get to England to see my dear ones after six years absence, we took the opportunity to travel by air with the French (although homeless)… and now to you.

We visited Lisa almost at once although I had very little hope of finding her here and there I found her where I had left her, busy sewing, Baby grown into a lovely long legged terribly clever miss. She was more than glad to see us, welcomed us to stay with her. We were to have left within (a few) days for Riva Bella but decided not to go.

You can be proud of your Lisa, Richard. She has had to work hard through these awful war years without you. They have suffered hunger and bitter cold, and bombardments. The four houses of the block next door to you is a ruin. She has been lonely and once very ill too but through it all her love for you has remained unchanged and now she is so excited and happy at the thought to returning to you...

Gustave may have judged this draft a little too forthright to be sent. A reply from Richard was written to Gustave, although addressed to both of them:

9th September 1945
Dear Gustl
Thank you very much for your letter of 21st July. I am writing to you although this letter is just as well meant for Marjorie but it is simpler to write to one person...You can ask Lisa how many times I wrote to her and asked her what had happened to you and Marjorie and knowing that you had been in the Sahara, I wondered what had eventually happened to you. So you can imagine that I was very glad when I heard that you were both safe and well and I was pleased to receive your letter which was most interesting.

I can imagine how bad it has been for you both during the war and I often thought, how Marjorie did not want to see what was going to happen and how many times I had said how she will regret all these happenings. I would have been very glad to have been wrong, all these things would have been saved to us, but unfortunately the whole outcome was unavoidable. Well we all have to be glad that it is over in this way although my poor sister and mother are both victims of this war and I can only hope that they did not suffer too much and too long...

As for your coming out here, I think as Gentiles you and Marjorie being British it should be easier. If I can do anything for you from here I would be only too glad. If you come out here first alone, you can stay with Lisa and me and I am sure you will find soon a job. Please enquire what you have to do to get the permit for permanent residency here. Any guarantee that is necessary I shall gladly give you.

In any case whatever the situation is, I am sure you will be able to earn a living here and it is much better to be here than to be in Europe where the situation will be difficult for a long time. The life here is pleasant and agreeable and although you miss a lot theatre and concerts and other things, you have an easy and nice life here in other ways.

I congratulate you on your little daughter and you know it seems unbelievable that Graham is already 17, a big grown up boy and when I left he was only a child.

Please think about these matters and let me know your point of view as soon as possible.

With best regards to Marjorie, I am

Yours sincerely

Signed Richard Steinhardt

There were so many options, but paramount to Marjorie was the need to see her parents. She was also missing Graham and of course was desperate to introduce the baby to her mother. Six long years – it seemed a lifetime. She had of course let them know about the baby's birth, but letters had been generally few and far between. Now her priority was to make that trip to England.

Food was in short supply and prices were sky high. Worst of all, the French authorities did not allow

Gustave a work permit, having classified him as stateless. They paid scant regard to his newly acquired Czech passport, let alone his ongoing claim for French nationality. He even possessed a letter from the firm he had worked for in Lyon whilst hiding in the unoccupied zone of France. Their main factory in Paris offered him employment in his previous capacity with a monthly salary of 5,500 Francs. Without a work permit Gustave was unable to accept this offer of a fresh start. It was a bitter blow, which left him disillusioned and dispirited.

Although relieved to be back in France, a draft letter dated August 1945 on a Ginzkey order book gives his own insight into the pull of the firm which he felt so much a part of:

> Dear Erik,
> At long last I am able to write to you and tell you a little of what we have gone through these last weeks. I am with my family back to France since a month. We could no longer watch the terrible things that happened in M[affersdorf]. On the first peace day we were bombarded. Happily our house was not damaged. Then we have lived weeks which I cannot describe you now. As with my French military papers I had the chance to be repatriated to France, we packed up all our furniture, locked it up into the rooms and left as quickly as we could. On that day a great number of people were fetched and I am afraid they will have to go nearly all. We had a very nice journey by airplane to Lyon but with all the formalities and waiting we were so glad when we at last arrived in Paris.
> Having no flat we went to friends for the first days. Now we have been lucky to meet a friend who will leave soonly for South Africa and let us have this flat which is a great sorrow less. My wife with baby are waiting for a visa to go to England to her parents to get some rest. My big boy is already in England since a fortnight and I am so glad

he will have an English passport and not have to suffer what we had with…

Our small boy could go to a Colonie de Vacances in the Centre of France and is staying with a nice family. I shall wait to see how things in Maff. settle down and whether our factory will continue to work as before. If so I shall go back in a month or two in the hope to take up my old job and come to your countries again. I am very much afraid that exportation won't start so quickly…

Gustave goes on to explain how expensive life in Paris has become and requests parcels of basic foodstuffs, mentioning again his difficulty without cigarettes:

I suppose you have not any more cigarettes than we – four a day. I shall try to have some sent from England…

If you have an opportunity I should be much obliged if you would ask whether there is a possibility for me to get a job as I must not count too much upon Ginzkey.

For Gustave, being jobless was soul destroying. The earlier offer from Ginzkey, even though it was in the Russian zone, became harder and harder to resist.

CHAPTER NINETEEN

AN ENGLISH WELCOME TURNS SOUR

Marjorie was so desperate not to have to return to Maffersdorf that she took a leaf out of Pierre's book. It was important for her now to get to England as soon as possible to see her family again after all these years. In a flash of inspiration, she had an idea to make some money which would justify the cost of such an expedition to Gustave. His rule of thrift had sustained them through the war and also enabled their return to Paris but now, times were becoming very hard indeed. So she decided to venture in her own small way into the import/export business. Her resourcefulness as a businesswoman proved a saving grace. Marjorie entered the *black market*.

The most popular perfume, Chanel No.5 had become very hard to find since the GIs, when war ended, had cleared most of the department stores of all their stock. The same was the case in England. For a long time, it was unavailable, making it all the more sought after. So when the famous brand started to re-appear, this became Marjorie's inspiration.

She started with a few bottles of the less expensive brands of French perfume from the cheapest source of supply, decanting it into tiny bottles which would sell in England for a healthy profit. She reserved the very costly Chanel No. 5 for the rare opportunities which surprisingly did occasionally arise. This idea was extended to anything which was exclusively French which would have a market in England, still governed by rations and austerity. They had to be small enough either to post or go into her luggage without attracting the attention of Customs & Excise.

Her departure was delayed because of her own passport, by now Czech. This was first issued in Paris in 1937 and renewed there in June 1945. Until she could reinstate her British passport, she was obliged to travel on a visitor's visa, for which delays were inevitable.

James, meanwhile, as part of his repatriation was sent with a group of boys to the French countryside at Rochechouart with the help of the *Comite des Oeuvres Sociales de la Resistance*. They were to be there for a month or more during July and August to fatten up and recuperate. He was 12 years old and Marjorie took him to join the others at the station where they were to begin their journey. On arrival in Rochechouart, they were taken to the Market Place by bus. They were lined up whilst those who had volunteered to have the children began to pick them out. As he was waiting he heard the sound of hooves, and a horse-drawn cart rounded the corner into the Market Place. It belonged to a wealthy farming family. James was delighted to be chosen by them. He enjoyed helping with the hay making and befriended a girl who lived close by.

While James was settled, it was agreed that Graham would go on ahead to England. Arrangements were made for him to stay with his grandparents at Severn Beach. Returning to England in the summer of 1945, Graham's emotions were mixed as he climbed down the steps of the military plane. He felt like a foreigner to this country; despite knowing he belonged, he knew so little of England. During the journey he wondered how Will and Lily would receive him. They were virtual strangers. He had last seen them in 1937 for a short visit during the school holidays when he was just nine years old. During that time he had stayed with Aunty Olive, of whom he had much clearer memories. She had three children; one of them, Rena, was exactly his age and Graham recalled going with her to school for a week or two before their holidays started.

Now he worried about his poor English. 'Will my German accent be a barrier? Will I be able to get a job?' he wondered.

His first port of call was a Rehabilitation Centre near London, where he was kept for a few days with others who had been stranded abroad since the outbreak of the war. One evening he was given half a crown so that he could go to the local cinema with the others. The experience was different from any film show he had seen during the war. German occupation had limited the availability and supply of any forms of entertainment other than those laid on for the armed forces, but even in wartime, London had far more to offer. Newly released films from Hollywood, even the style and size of the cinema, were in excess of anything one could imagine in a little village like Maffersdorf.

At the Rehabilitation Centre they were thoroughly examined by a doctor and a medical history was compiled. They were encouraged to shower every day – another new experience. They had their hair cut and were given some new clothes. Finally, they were given several pound notes and some small change with an explanation of their value. Then with a good luck wish and directions as to how to travel to their relatives, they were sent off.

Full of trepidation and excitement, Graham boarded a double-decker bus and watched the hustle and bustle of the London traffic. At Paddington Station he had to ask for his railway ticket three times before the man understood him. But his spirits lifted as he discovered a new found confidence; he was determined that he would soon learn to speak the language of his mother country.

The journey by train to Bristol took over three hours. From Bristol he had to change for Severn Beach. While only half an hour away, he knew there would be nobody to meet him. Graham had been unable to notify his grandparents; a home telephone was the preserve of the elite. It was with some apprehension that he made his own way to No. 20 Beach Avenue.

His reception was cool. Grandpa seemed oblivious to what Graham and the family had been through. He was nearing retirement now and his bluntness had not mellowed with age. Grandma, only one month older, seemed much more frail at 65. She still appeared very ladylike to Graham, who appreciated her gentle kindness and finesse all the more given Will's insensitivity.

Grandpa's pride and joy was a monstrous billiard table which almost filled the front room. It was customary for the front room to be reserved for special occasions and in this house it was only used for Sunday family gatherings. His sons would take him to the pub and then indulge him with a game of billiards, while the wives stayed in the living room exchanging gossip with Grandma whilst they made tea together.

The British reserve which had been bred into his grandfather through generations of Victorian example came as a shock to Graham. A stiff upper lip was the order of the day; for a man to show any trace of emotion was perceived as a sign of weakness. Grandpa's outlet was his wit, which had stood him in good stead with friends and family throughout his life. This was rather lost on Graham, partly due to the language but also the huge culture gap.

Grandpa's escape from introspection and a perfect way to avoid deep and meaningful conversation was the billiard table. He spent many hours around the table with Graham, teaching him the rules of engagement and instilling the fear of God lest he should damage the green baize surface. Not once did he sit down to talk to the boy, let alone ask any questions about the war years or about the family.

After a week or two, Grandpa was showing signs of impatience. 'Isn't it time you thought about getting a job? You won't be able to loaf around, you know. You have had your citizenship given to you. Our boys at your age were down the coal mines as Bevin Boys. That was their part in the war effort.'

Coal mining held little appeal for Graham so he remained quiet. He was aware that he was outstaying his welcome, partly due to his own behaviour. He could be arrogant and argumentative. His experiences to date meant that the adolescent conviction that he knew everything far better than his elders was particularly entrenched. His German accent and general cockiness grated on his grandfather, who sometimes referred to him as 'a little Nazi', enraging Graham, who one day retaliated: 'How can you call me that? Why do you think I deserted? Do you have no idea of the risks I've taken to get away from the Nazis? I've seen more action than you!'

'How dare you speak to me like that?!' roared the old man.

'I dare because I speak as a man and a soldier and so as your equal! If I'm man enough to fight in that war, I won't be treated as a child here!'

'You're under my roof, boy! You should be looking for a job and paying for your keep! Listen to that accent – bring that language into my house, you can damn well show some respect. Free board and lodging to loaf around all day? If you're a man, get a job!'

As time went on, his grandfather became more irritable at the very sight of him. Graham did his best to keep out of his way and never to appear unoccupied, but the entire household was under a shadow; he would have to move on.

It was a huge relief to Graham to hear that his mother and siblings were at last on their way to England. Marjorie had such high expectations for this trip. Graham recalled how she had often expressed her regret during the war years at the hurt she'd caused her parents by leaving home so early and going to Paris. Of course, he mused, marrying a Sudeten German Czech would not have helped. As far as Marjorie's father were concerned, Gustave was 'a Kraut' and that was that.

Marjorie and the children were finally granted a return visa to England on 28th August. On 7th September 1945 they arrived at Severn Beach. It was their first visit since 1937; for the baby, just a week from her first birthday, it was the first time ever. On this occasion, the whole family was there to meet them at the station. Everyone walked back up the road, chatting happily and cooing at the baby. The little procession passed the row of shops in front of the sea wall and turned up the tree lined Avenue to Grandma and Grandpa's house at No. 20.

After eight long years, Marjorie was home with her beloved mother and her family. There was great initial excitement, but it was short-lived. The house was indeed very small. Graham's presence was testing Grandpa to the limits. The prospect of a further three people in his home including a squalling baby, dirty nappies and endless baggage had caused friction between Will and Lily even before they arrived. Once reality set in, it all became too much. Marjorie and the children left the Beach after only a few days.

She was heartbroken. Tears streamed down her face as they departed then made the long journey by train to her sister Mona in Hertfordshire. The journey was punctuated with spells of attending to the baby and entertaining the boys. The latter felt more of a necessity for her than for them; she tried desperately to lift her spirits. Marjorie was devastated. Once the initial excitement was over, her family had shown absolutely no interest in her at all. During all those years of war and hardship she had yearned to talk to them but once they were finally together there was just far too much going on. Turning it over and over in her mind, she stared bleakly out of the window at the tired-looking English countryside. The summer was drawing to a close.

She recalled all the years of keeping secrets from Gustave to send their monthly payments. Marjorie had hoped that she could turn to her parents and the wider family now that she and Gustave were in need. Although they were no longer well off and money had sparked the dissent, it was the lack of moral support which weighed most heavily. In a fit of pique, her father had offered to pay it all back, but she knew they could never afford it so did not open the discussion again.

The train jolted to a stop, bringing her back to the present. Marjorie tried to reason with herself: the war had left its mark on everyone and they too had been through very hard times. But how could they begin to imagine the horrors of her own war, or Graham's?

All they knew was that he had been called up at sixteen to fight for Hitler. They could only see him, with his youthful arrogance, as 'a little Nazi'.

'If only they had given me the chance to explain to them,' she fretted as the train rumbled on. 'If only they knew – not just about Graham's escape but about Gustave; how he gave himself up to starvation and torture in a Concentration Camp, rather than fight against my brothers.'

The lost opportunity made her heart ache. She knew that her mother would have wanted much more but was powerless to stand up to the man she so loved. Marjorie did understand; she loved them both very much. She struggled to hold back the tears in front of the children, especially Graham who knew exactly what she was feeling. From time to time during that journey she simply had to let the tears flow, at one point drawing the baby into her arms to stifle her own sobs.

As the train rattled on, the children began to stir. Marjorie faced a very uncertain future. With an effort, she marshalled her thoughts. First and foremost, Graham must be launched on a career path and settled in England. For herself, Gustave and the younger children, she had a plan in mind, at least for the short term. 'Perhaps, England may not be for us after all?' she wondered.

If Gustave were not allowed to work in France, then could she persuade him? As much as they both loved Paris, they had little or no means of regular income. They had used most of their savings. There was probably not enough to last until he could gain French nationality, so they must look at alternatives.

England now held little attraction for her, especially given her family's indifference. What about the Steinhardts in South Africa? Lisa would soon join her husband and she would be able to give her friend a frank assessment of life over there.

It was a tempting prospect: a sunny warm climate and a new beginning. Although Gustave had shrunk from the mere suggestion of it, Marjorie had not yet dismissed the idea and as she stared out of the train window, she thought she could persuade him. His parents were now gone and the ties with her own seemed all but broken, so the distance would not be that dreadful. Perhaps there would be opportunities for the whole family, even Graham.

They changed trains at Paddington. Soon they were sitting comfortably with Mona, her husband John and son Raymond at their home in Puckeridge. Raymond was a few years younger than Graham but they soon got chatting, James joining in whenever his limited English would allow. Once the children were in bed, conversation between the adults went on late into the night.

Marjorie asked Mona and John if they would be willing to take Graham for a few weeks and help him find a job. Convinced that his fluent French and German would enable him to provide language tuition, Marjorie wrote an advertisement to be placed in the local newspapers. The two sisters happily discussed their planned business, analysing the items which would sell just to friends and neighbours.

The tiny bottles of perfume turned out to be in great demand. Marjorie also discovered that nylon stockings were much cheaper in England. She bought as many pairs as her limited funds would allow her to take back to Paris.

She felt quite pleased with herself as they made their farewells to Mona and John. They spent a few days in Southampton with Olive before boarding the ferry.

One matter had dominated the snippets of private conversation Marjorie had managed to have with her mother, and later with Mona. There had been a double tragedy in Olive's life in the last two years of the war. First, she had lost her eldest daughter Betty, aged twenty-one, to tuberculosis. Soon afterwards, Olive had contracted the disease herself. Although the doctors were confident of a full recovery, she was so badly affected by her grief that she opted to have the infected lung removed.

A full year had passed since Olive's operation by the time of Marjorie's visit. She had recovered well physically, although the emotional scars were still healing from Betty's loss. Her spirits had lifted when she received Marjorie's letter asking if she could bring the children to stay. Soon the sisters were chatting and laughing as though they had seen each other yesterday. Once more, when the children were tucked up in bed, various options were held up this way and that. While talking would not bring an instant solution, Olive's counsel was greatly appreciated in those few hours.

Marjorie's main concern at this point was for James. She felt strongly that their circumstances in Paris, both financially and emotionally, were fragile and that he deserved better. It was also very important to her that he should be able to master the English language, which had not been given priority during the years in Maffersdorf. The intervening weeks in Paris had only served to exacerbate the problem, so she discussed with Olive the possibility of his staying in England and starting the new school year in Southampton.

Marjorie knew that Olive was still not strong enough to take on this extra responsibility, but together they came up with the answer. Aunt Liz was a teacher herself and also lived in Southampton. Marjorie admired her aunt greatly and felt sure she would understand. She caught the bus over to her aunt's house the next day and told her everything that had happened.

Aunt Liz was Grandpa's sister. She did not share his brusque personality. In fact, she and her brother, also a teacher, had never quite understood Will's choice of a career on the shop floor. He had evidently had the brain to pursue a profession, but now they were poles apart. Perhaps mindful of her failure to assist Marjorie when she last wrote to her with the investment opportunity, this time Aunt Liz did not hesitate. She said yes, on one condition: that James could spend some weekends with Olive. That lady readily agreed.

James was surprised and disappointed to be left behind. Marjorie promised him faithfully that she and his sister would return to England in a few weeks and certainly by Christmas. He settled down quickly to a new school and total immersion in the English language. James became very fond of Olive. They were kindred spirits. For now, he counted the weeks until he would see his own family again.

Marjorie boarded the ferry with only her daughter and a heavy heart. Her family was split once again. At just a year old, the baby's needs were enough to keep her occupied, but once she settled into her seat and the baby slept she was once again alone with her thoughts.

It was a very bad crossing. Marjorie had arrived in Southampton without her overcoat which she'd left at Mona's and there had not been enough time to send it on to Olive. To make matters worse, a porthole was open and she got drenched before someone came to close it. When they disembarked in Le Havre, she got through safely with all of her parcels. Gustave was waiting. Marjorie was cold, wet and exhausted; it was a relief that they were able to board the rail connection to Paris without much of a wait.

'I've missed you so much,' said Gustave. 'And what about our boys?'

She had so much to tell him. Marjorie talked for the entire journey, careful not to mention how the trip to her parents had ended. Despite her own feelings, she couldn't bear him to think badly of them. She was so thankful to be back.

CHAPTER TWENTY

HER LADYSHIP'S TUTOR

By October they had left the small apartment which had been their first refuge on their return to Paris. The rent, though low, had become unaffordable so they welcomed the move into the tiny apartment with Lisa Steinhart while she waited for her visa. 'Please make it your home for as long as you need,' she said. Marjorie was grateful to have a roof over their heads but felt still more destabilised: yet another move. When she thought of her beautiful Paris apartment just a few years ago, it felt like someone else's charmed life. She struggled to believe in an end to the war, let alone a return to that kind of prosperity.

Small though it was, they all got on very well but Marjorie was yearning for James. His month in the countryside had been hard enough but now the Channel lay between them. She was used to long absences from Graham, and in any case accepted that he was now a man and able to look after himself, but for James it was different. He was a child far away from home.[23]

On her thirty ninth birthday, 26th October 1945, Marjorie wrote to Mona. The letter was full of her sadness at 'how bitter the disappointment of my homecoming had been'. She mentioned a Mr Filmer, who 'offered me the first helping hand out of religious goodness and this is why I have sent Graham to him'.

Mona replied shortly afterwards, offering to have Graham stay in their home on his return from Mr Filmer.

Marjorie replied gratefully at once:

> Poor love, he <u>is</u> only seventeen and wants already to manage alone but I want <u>nothing</u> to be done in a hurry. I ask you to keep him with you until he has found something suitable. I would like you to put an Ad. in the personal or Educational [column] of the Telegraph or Times:
>
> **Young gentleman perfect French and German, music, sport, hobby-loving, seeks tutor post to young children of excellent family**
>
> 'I am so sorry that the days were so short but poor Gustave was longing for our return, my presence being necessary to obtain the papers for Tzchecoslovakia. And then I needed him too, badly, he being the only real person in a world all fallen to pieces but we are going to try to come again. We have already made, today, our demand for the Visa'.

Their great friends Maria and Pierre were even persuaded to join them in a proposed Christmas trip. They set about exploring their own chances of gaining a visa.

---

[23] In fact, James had little recollection of this interlude, his memory clouded by the events which followed.

The perennial difficulty of travel proved almost insurmountable. Marjorie requested Mona's help regarding the re-issue of her English passport. This had not been arranged during her trip as she had been unable to get to London. As time went on, she was concerned that they would not be able to afford the trip home for Christmas. Marjorie set about doing all she could to earn and save, but the all-important return trip to Czechoslovakia was causing her the greatest worry. She wrote to Graham to tell him that she was planning to send Auntie Mona a *volmacht* – full authority to act on their behalf.

>...It may seem stupid, but one never knows and you are not yet *volljahrig* (of age). If within six months of our departure nothing should be heard of us, Auntie Mona has the right to remove Auntie Mariechen's jewels from the safe at Lloyds. If you will do your best to get in touch with them later at the Werdau address of 1 Ottostrasse.
>
>I am leaving my own bijoux!! which must later be for Baby and if really, I am not able to get out, Auntie Mona will ask solicitor friends of hers to write stating that the furniture is my private property as an Englishwoman – and you must leave no peace until you get it over to England.
>
>I am terrified of this voyage, yet it must be done to get our home out. It would seem theatrical to someone else if I were to tell them, but you know that country and the danger for everyone. I only hope we get out safely. In any case, I want to tell you how happy I am to know <u>you</u> are happy there as well as Jim, there in my country and out of danger.
>
>Think sometimes of your Mama kindly, the last years have been so unkind to me. It was all so different from what I had planned. I am missing you very much and only hope that I can get over for Christmas to you all to have a little sunshine again. Do write to me my dear. Tell me all

about your new life. Try to get up to a theatre or a nice concert sometimes. How I dreamed to do all this with you. How too sad is life. How I pray that you will have it differently. Write to me soon. My thoughts are very often with you although I have so little time for me to write to you.

    Goodnight my love, Your Mama

Graham was distressed to read his mother's words, so full of fear and foreboding. It was obvious that his father had persuaded her that a return to Maffersdorf was essential to organise the collection of their 'home': furniture and other household contents which, five years earlier, had been returned through the kindness of Peter, the German officer in Paris, and safely stored by his father's faithful employers. The plan was to have everything forwarded to England from where they could then obtain the visas for South Africa. But Graham knew his father well enough to realise that he wouldn't have the courage to leave Europe. England, maybe; but a whole new continent, 5,500 miles away? No, Gustave was relying on a job offer which Marjorie would agree was too good to refuse, and a new atmosphere in Maffersdorf which would prove welcoming in reality – a far cry from the fearsome place which she so dreaded.

    Graham's long letter in reply to his mother reveals a wisdom and compassion unusual for a boy of seventeen, as well as an impressive new command of his mother tongue.

    Hertford Nov 24th (1945)
    My dear, dear Mummy
    This morning we received your so sad letter. You must be in a terrible state, you, poor Mummy. If only I was there with you to console you a little. I would give anything to

be able to be with you and stay with you during the whole journey. You must have been very down with your nerves when you wrote that letter. You must not be so silly and worry yourself about your imaginations. It won't be as bad as that in any way. I think I know just as much as you do about the land. It certainly is not the nicest place to be in if one has been a Nazi but we – we are known all over the place. You have got all the Baraque French boys and Babs, Fred and so on to stand for you <u>if</u> anything should go wrong. But no, there is no need to worry yourself to such an extent. You would have frightened me to death with that letter if I didn't know how courageous and clever you are. <u>You</u> will come out everywhere victorious and you have had to do with much worse people than those!! And when you are still here we shall, both Jim and I, pray every night for you and I would fight until I would succeed if anything should turn wrong. But it will not dear, don't worry! Oh what would I give to be able to go through it with you.

This morning I had a letter from Mr Filmer again. I write to him as often as I can. I will enclose one of his cards and hope that you will receive this letter before leaving. I hope it will help you to pick yourself up. I am proud that I have made friends everywhere I went, and friends that really think I am worth to be your son Mummy dear, I always wanted and will not stop til I can show you that your hopes were not all only hopes unfulfilled that every mother has for her children.

I will go to the De Havillands and see there if I cannot get the education as an engineer. The job that I have got now is very nice because I am learning something that will always bring me some money if I haven't got anything but I do not intend to stay. I will still find something where your Graham will come out as something. If I went on with the books I would have to be a Librarian and that – well I'm not so keen because it will [not] be able to pay enough. I am also earning 35/- a week for the beginning so I am looking out for something better.

I have come together with very nice people that have lived 15 years in Paris and now through the war have been forced to return here. The wife is French and the husband is English so they have established themselves in a very big house in Hertford where they live with their three children. Of course they are first class people! Their home is I think being sent over to England. I think too that it would be best if you came to stay here until we are as far from the big wandering out[24].

I am so longing to see you and Baby again that I am already preparing everything for Xmas. If only I had a lot of money to buy you something really nice! But that will come soon too.

I wonder whom you will find still in Maff. and Reich. If you get there sooner than I think then write at once. The past does go, doesn't it. If you see the Valenta's give them all my love and, of course, to everyone too. I wonder if Harold is home? Please do write even if you have so much to do. I am waiting always for news and I will be frightened if you do let me go without hearing. So please do. I will leave everything to answer. Oh if only I could go with you!!! How is the baby? Is she already talking? French?

So do not despair, our thoughts and prayers are and shall always be with you. I will have to stop now because it is really getting too late and too long, so let me kiss you goodbye and all the luck I can with you.

Loving Graham

Ps When you come back we shall have the loveliest Christmas ever had.

In the meantime, John and Mona's garden nursery could offer little work for Graham through the winter months. It had not come easily to him in any case.

---

[24] The expulsion of the Germans from Czechoslovakia see p.280

His letter to his mother speaks of his ambitions to find work that will make her proud of him. For a short time, he had found a job with a German Jewish couple called the Romers, who had managed to get away from Germany just in time before the war and found asylum in England. Mr Romer was a book restorer with a shop in which he sold fine old leather-bound books. They proved to be just the kind of people that Graham needed: kind, educated and far more understanding of the difficulties Graham was facing than his English relatives. More importantly, they could converse in German. They found him a room nearby and put him to work on Mrs Romer's side of the business, making leather purses, briefcases and other items. Graham was not sad to leave his Aunt's house. He was keen to learn and had a good eye for precision. His lady employer was very pleased with him and his confidence began to grow.

At the same time, several letters were passing between Marjorie and Mona from October to December 1945. The general tone was of the struggle to obtain the paperwork required to get them back to England. She asked for John's help in writing to the Home Office to explain their situation, in the hope that this would facilitate both Marjorie's English passport and the much needed visa for Gustave. Hopes for Christmas with her boys were fading fast when she wrote the following to Mona:

> ...Really Gustave has had such a rotten time I would not have the courage to spend time without him – perhaps before or afterwards but not just at Xmas. We have all our papers in order for Tczechoslovakia and think within a fortnight to leave. We are waiting for the air service to start as the train journey takes 3 days and Baby could not stand

this, or I either. We are slowly getting over our colds from the English return journey.

Before I go, I am going to write you a paper today that if anything happens to Gustave or me whilst there, that you have the right to use the key of the safe I have here at Lloyds. You are the only member of my family that I really feel I can trust in this matter. The key I shall leave at Lambrechts or Maria's. This too I will let you know. Graham is under age. I too, will ask you if there should be any complications there, one never knows, to ask your solicitor friends to write me an official statement that I took my furniture from England in 1932 to France and that it is my personal belongings. All this is probably stupidity on my part but in such a corner of Europe one can really never know and I shall not be happy until my things are either here or in England. Mr Filmer has not been able to get a priority billet (ticket) for our airplace but, in any case, we cannot come for Xmas. In the worst case, we shall come either before or after so that we can bring everything back.

Lots of fond love, Marjorie

In the meantime, Marjorie's contacts in the Visa Department had paid off to assist her friend Lisa Steinhardt. She and her daughter were ready, at last, to join Richard in South Africa.

In her next letter to Mona dated 10th December 1945 Marjorie thanks John for his to the Home Secretary:

> …Our hopes for Christmas have sunk very low my dear. If things were nicer I would say why don't you come over instead. You could pay your voyage by bringing some things, and room we have. It is nothing like Neuilly of course but Lisa has left everything we needed. God bless her. She left among tears on Tuesday for a happy land. They leave Lisbonne on the 15th.

Lisa's departure had only reinforced Marjorie's hopes for a new life in the sunshine. The same letter opens with the following lines:

> Dear Mo, dear John,
> John's letter reached us on Saturday and we thank him sincerely for his kindness. Let us hope that it will have some result that will enable us to wait in England, instead of here, the formalities necessary for our departure for South Afrika...

Suddenly, there was a response to Marjorie's advertisement. Graham was appointed to teach the young family of some titled aristocrats, the Lees, who lived in an impressive Tudor mansion called Old Chestnut House in Lower Moor near Evesham. There he was introduced to little Lady Margaret and her brother. He was shocked to be asked to teach the children in all subjects and made sure to explain his inexperience, but they liked him immediately.

The school year was in progress and the children had not been out of formal education for long. Graham was quick to prepare himself. He procured a school curriculum and tried to ascertain the children's level. He took his task very seriously. The children, to his dismay, did not. After a battle, however, he won them over and they got on well together.

Graham did not fare so well with the gentleman of the house who ran an officers' club for men from the nearby military air base and drank heavily. He could be the most well-mannered and thoughtful person when he wished to be, but could act like a raving maniac at other times, thought Graham. He treated his very sweet, ladylike wife abominably. The young tutor, unable to hide his discomfort over this, invoked her husband's wrath towards him.

Graham retired to his room as much as he could. He prepared his lessons, spent the teaching time in a separate room and enjoyed going for walks and tree climbing expeditions with the children. At night, however, there was a lot of noise and carousing.

Once, in the middle of the night, someone rushed into his room. Graham awoke with a start and switched on the light. There stood a lady stark naked, with a glass of champagne in her hand; a sight he had so far never seen. When she saw him she let out a cry and ran out again.

The next evening he was sitting with the lady of the house and told her about the incident. She laughed and said, 'Probably that husband of mine was after her.' She smiled. 'Why did you let her go?'

'My mother says I am a bit backward in these matters, but she has great confidence in me otherwise,' Graham replied.

The longer he was there, the more he felt as though he was in a mad-house. In his spare time he developed a hobby. One of the Air Force men who came to the club brought along a small scale model of a Spitfire he had made of Perspex. Graham admired it and the officer offered to teach him to make one. He showed him how to saw the pieces out of a quarter-inch thick plate of Perspex and then how to work on them with a knife, files and sandpaper, finally polishing the model with toothpaste. It became quite a passion; Graham built them so well that the officers bought them as quickly as he could make them.

On one occasion he had placed a few finished models of different planes on the grand piano in the big room where the bar was, so that the club members could look at them. His Lordship lost his temper and threw a book across the room. It hit the delicate little planes and swept them off the piano. They were in pieces. Furious, Graham gave his notice.

He taught the children until the end of the month. Her Ladyship cried and pleaded with him to stay. When he packed his bags and hugged the children, she came and kissed Graham in a way he had never been kissed before. She was such an unhappy woman, he felt guilty leaving her.

His Lordship refused to pay Graham. 'You have broken your contract. You will not receive your salary. Goodbye and good riddance!'

Crestfallen, Graham returned briefly to Aunt Olive in Southampton. He considered carefully why things weren't working out for him. First Grandpa, then Auntie Mona and now this. It had all started so well but gradually he was realising that life, even in peacetime, was going to mean a big adjustment. If only he could make a living from photography. That was his great love, but he couldn't even afford to buy a camera. Graham was determined to make his parents proud of him somehow. He would find a way.

CHAPTER TWENTY-ONE

NO VISA FOR CHRISTMAS

Christmas came and went with no word from the Home Office. Gustave became more and more despondent. He maintained contact with Ginzkey and was comforted to hear that they still wanted him back in Maffersdorf to take a senior position. He knew Marjorie would not be pleased but urged her to give him the chance at least to hear them out. Perhaps one day it would get them back to their old life in Paris.

Marjorie managed to make another trip to England with her daughter (now 17 months) in February, but a wire from Gustave brought her visit to an abrupt end. On her return she wrote:

> Sunday 24th February 1946
> My dear John dear
> Here I am in Paris after a hectic end to my visit and am glad to be back, although disappointed not to have finished half of what I set out to do. I went down to Mother's last Saturday intending to spend until about Thursday there but telephoned to Gustave on Sunday night when he told me that Marie, his sister, had telegraphed urgently saying his presence was required to help them and that he had got

places in the plane for 28th. This, of course, upset all my plans. I left there on Tuesday morning, Father has bought a car – so of course my question could not be settled as I had wished. I intended coming up to London on Thursday and coming down to you on Friday to leave on Sat. But as luck would have it, I tried to get my ticket in Southampton at Cooks who, to my surprise, told me that there was <u>no</u> boat at all on Saturday and only the one leaving Sunday, Victoria at 10 – did not get to Paris till 5.30 also nearly 24 hours on the way, which I could not have faced with Baby.

So I got up to town on Thursday and went to Liz Binn's wanting from there to phone you whether you would come to the train with my things: but mess all the way. Things had gone all so quickly, I had not been able to let her know and when we got down there, worn out, we had the luck to find her out for the night and Harry ill. I went straight to bed and in the middle of the night came your wire. I just did not know what to think. I thought that Gustave was afraid of the gales and as I had my ticket and you know, one has to reserve beforehand, I just left thinking we were leaving on Thursday for Maffersdorf but we think to leave a little later about the 12th of March and so my coat had better stay with you. I shall come back to England afterwards. I am heartbroken about it as it is the only decent thing I have left.

Mo dear, will you be a dear and send me Miss Sargeant's money. I am posting this in a thickish envelope for you to see. I sent two notes a time in an envelope like this per airmail, and all is safe, so if you would send every second day for the next fortnight. Stamps of course go on my account. Thank you a thousand times too for having helped me with the solicitor's letter.

The Home Office told me as Graham is British all his possessions are protected by the Crown. There is no need for me to be afraid for our things but I want to be certain. I have still a lot to tell you and will write again but now get this off or I will be too late.

Love to all
Margie…*Love to you all Gustave*

The following letter was written and posted on 1st March:

> 90 Chemin de la Fouilliere,
> Suresnes
>
> Dear Mo,
> I am writing this letter in haste as we have just heard that we have places in the plane for Tuesday. We have very nice news in so far that we have, after all, received our visas for exit <u>and</u> return…

More follows about perfumes, stockings, money and so on. At the foot of the letter is written:

> Dear Mona and John,
> I knew your telegram would not arrive in time, but still, I was glad when Marjorie and Baby arrived at St Lazare. Baby is quite alright again and I hope she will be alright for the next journey on Tuesday. Today it was snowing and if this continues all night we shall not be able to go out of the house tomorrow morning. Thank you again, Dears, for all you have done for Marj and Baby and hoping to be able to give you soon good news from Czechosl. I am, with love to you all.
> Gustave

The envelope was stamped *Posted 16.30 3 46 PARIS 81* on *1st March 1946.*

In the preceding weeks Graham had sought refuge with Aunt Olive after the debacle in Worcestershire. She was kind and he enjoyed her sense of fun. They laughed a great deal as he related his recent adventures. His experiences with Mona and Grandpa, however, had left their mark. Graham knew he must find work, but he still felt like a foreigner. There was little chance of finding work near Ashurst, so he tried in Southampton where he was amazed at the way he was treated in all official places.

In spite of his accent, ladies at the Labour Exchange went out of their way to be helpful. He felt as though he was in a different world and was very grateful to be a British subject. It was a relief to realise that he couldn't be all that bad after all. Perhaps things were looking up.

He tried one or two jobs but quickly gave up on them. A friend of the Bennetts took him out one day in a rowing boat on Southampton water.

'Why don't you try your luck in America?' one of them suggested. 'You could stow away on one of the big liners. It's quite easy on those huge floating hotels. Ever been on the Queen Elizabeth? You should see the luxury! The Americans are very helpful. You should find it easier there because they have so many immigrants who can't speak good English.' Graham decided to try it.

For all her enterprising spirit, he knew that Marjorie would not have approved. Gustave would have been horrified. Graham managed to get on board the Queen Mary and hid in a closet where piles of blankets were kept. It was dark and uncomfortable and he began to have second thoughts. Hours seemed to pass and he kept thinking, 'How much longer before this ship leaves at last?'

Suddenly the door opened, someone took out some blankets and he was discovered. Graham was ordered out and taken to the purser who was very stern. Two seamen took charge of Graham, marching him off the ship.

'Where are you taking me?' he asked.

'To the police station, lad.'

He was contemplating running away when a big man who was passing asked, 'What has he been up to?'

The sailors answered, 'Stowaway'.

The man turned out to be the captain of a trawler. Turning to Graham, he said, 'You're no kid any more. Do you want to go to sea? If you do, I have a place for you in my crew. Who knows, we might be able to make an able seaman out of you.'

'If these two will let me, I'll come.'

The captain gave them a wink and they handed him over. Irresistibly drawn to the idea of such adventure, Graham almost had to pinch himself in disbelief. His head was spinning at this new change of course. One minute he was heading for a police cell, the next he was being offered a new chapter in his life. He couldn't wait to tell his Aunt.

He signed on, bade farewell to Aunt Olive and moved into his small portion of the crew's quarters; a rather smelly bunk and a narrow wardrobe to stow his clothes. He was shown the different parts of the small cargo vessel, including the galley where he would take his turn to cook for the crew – a daunting prospect! His only experience of cooking had been frying hamsters and squirrels in the FLAK. The look on his face was not lost on the sailor who was showing him around, who said, 'It's OK, we'll teach you!'

Then the deck had to be scrubbed. Graham found his way around: the bridge where he would be on duty, steering the vessel under the Captain's orders, and the hold, which he would help load and unload by means of a crane.

He liked the Captain immediately. But the crew of six, beside himself, were all Scotsmen who had been at sea all their lives. They were short on talk and broad in accent.

They sailed on a perfect day, blue sky and a calm sea. Graham felt on top of the world at the helm, steering the vessel around the Isle of Wight and into the open sea. Once he'd got the feel of the speed and the boat responding to the wheel changing direction, he proudly echoed the Captain's orders, 'South South West, 12 knots'.

This felt great. The Captain asked him lots of questions so Graham told him some of his story. He thought things could not be better, until they rounded Cornwall and the sea got rough.

In the Irish Sea they experienced the first gales. The wind blew at Force 10, waves higher than houses. Very, very sick, Graham somehow managed his four hours at the wheel. He felt too ill to get out of his bunk when the bell sounded next and the men came and lifted him out.

Carrying him onto the deck, they told him the wind would give him back his spirits and held him by his feet over the railing, to save him vomiting over them.

'Terrible,' he groaned. 'Drop me – drowning can't be worse.' They laughed heartily, set him on his feet and sent him into the galley to prepare their next meal. The Captain said, 'It'll be alright, you'll soon get your sea legs, my lad!'

What bliss it was to get into port in Belfast and to place his feet on solid ground! They were paid – a fortune to them – and enjoyed the next day off duty.

'Find yourself a pretty girl,' they encouraged him. 'Don't get hooked by one of the pimps.'

He had vowed to sign off the first chance he got, but after a few days in port and money to spend with no restrictions, things looked very different. The Captain assured him once more, 'You'll get your sea legs and get over it'. Graham stayed on board and they sailed on to Scotland.

Leith was their next port of call. The weather didn't improve much; the Captain told Graham they'd have to steer near the Islands where it could be very treacherous. The Captain was out on the bridge in the wind and weather, watching intently for rocks with his binoculars and shouting orders. Graham needed to react quickly and accurately, which he did in spite of feeling sick.

They got through and the Captain said, 'Well, I'm proud of you! You'll make a good seaman. Just don't give up. Of course I know you won't stay with us all your life!'

As the sea sickness abated, Graham wondered whether this really could be a new chapter opening in his life. It was certainly one he'd never contemplated before. At least his accommodation would be catered for, and Aunty Olive could probably put up with him coming and going for a bit until he could save up some money. Would it make his parents proud of him, though? It was a world away from the household of Lord and Lady Lee.

There had been no time to write the usual newsy letter to his parents. Unbeknown to him, however, his brother was writing to them instead.

Dear Mummy and Daddy
I hope you had a good crossing. We have snow here and it is very cold. I am very happy here and in school. I had already 3 credits. I went since you went away once to the pictures. The next time I'll write a longer letter than this. How is Sylvia-Maria getting on? I've just heard from Aunty that you are not going to Czechoslovakia so soon as you thought.
Your Jimmy
Graham is going to Ireland on a ship today.
Aunty will tell you about it.

> 11 St (Ch) Catherines
> South hamton 11s
>
> Dear Mummy and
> Daddy,
>
> I hope you had a good cros-
> sing. We have snow here and
> it is very cold. I am very happy
> here and in school. I had
> already two Credits. I went
> since you went away once to
> the pictures. The next time I'll
> write a longer letter than this
> one. How is Sylvia Klara get-
> ting on? I just heard of Aunty
> that you are not going to
> (Ch) Czechoslovakia so soon as
> you thought.
>   your
>   Jimmy
>
> Graham is going to Ireland
> on a ship to-day. Aunty will
> tell you about it.

CHAPTER TWENTY-TWO

PRAGUE AIRSPACE
TUES. 5TH MARCH 1946

The plane circled in the blizzard for what seemed an age. Then to everyone's relief, they heard the engine noise change as if preparing to land. Visibility was so poor that the second pilot was obliged to open the window, but still they could see nothing. Thick fog made any visual observations impossible.

The runway suddenly appeared in view through the heavy snow, but they were approaching from the wrong angle. The plane came down broadside. The undercarriage smashed, the plane broke in two and the 2,000 litres of fuel on board caught fire.

The rear end was engulfed by flames. Gustave was killed instantly. As smoke crept through the plane Marjorie and the baby were still conscious. There were groans and cries of pain coming from one or two other passengers, but these gradually gave way to nothing but the sound of metal on metal, falling debris and the crying child.

Badly injured, Marjorie tried again and again to free herself. She had been holding the baby on her lap but the impact had thrown the little one on to the floor and now she couldn't reach her. Seeing that Jean was alive, Marjorie used all the strength she could muster, screaming at him to save her child.

The baby's little coat was alight, the flames crawling up her left arm. The tiny hand was already badly burnt. Unable to move and in terrible pain, Marjorie witnessed her sobbing child lurching from one piece of smouldering debris to another, flames devouring her coat. She despaired of her helplessness. Where on earth was Gustave? Why wasn't he here, right now, when she really needed him?

Still pinned to her seat, in an agony of fear and pain Marjorie watched Jean heave himself over jagged pieces of smouldering wreckage and gather up her child. In the absence of any sign of help from outside, he was her only hope. Knowing that the baby was alive, seeing her in his arms, Marjorie gave a sigh of relief before pain engulfed her.

Le Monde – *Past News* 6.3.1946

CHAPTER TWENTY-THREE

EYE WITNESS ACCOUNTS

The fate of Gustave and Marjorie's baby daughter was now in the hands of strangers.

Badly wounded with broken bones and an injured side, Jean nevertheless reacted exactly as he had been trained. He rolled the baby quickly in his overcoat, smothering the flames, and dragged himself and her along what remained of the gangway. There was a huge gash in the side of the plane, through which he forced them both out into the biting wind. The heavy snow cushioned first the baby's, then his own excruciating fall. He crawled, hauling the baby away from the plane, before the pain overwhelmed him. Only when Jean finally lost consciousness did he let go of the child.

Premysl Zantovski witnessed the whole dreadful scene as he waited to greet the family at the airport. He had travelled by express train to Prague-Ruzyne in order to welcome Gustave and Marjorie at the aerodrome and accompany them to Maffersdorf. He had waited and waited for the arrival of the plane, then an announcement had been made at 18.10.

Within six or seven minutes he was at the scene of the crash, together with the ground organisation and other people wanting to help if at all possible. The first pilot Balik, the second pilot and one other gentleman were rescued but died shortly afterwards from their injuries. Most of the 11 passengers and 4 crew had died in the crash. Jean and the baby were the only survivors. The baby was lying, still conscious and not crying, near the left wing of the plane. Zantovski did not recognise her at first, the little face black from smoke. The baby was taken to the military hospital of Stechovice near Prague and he continued to help with the rescue work for some time.

By the time Zantovski arrived at Stechovice at midnight, he was told that the baby had been transferred to the children's hospital in Prague. Rushing from one hospital to the other, he eventually found her in the children's hospital at Karlov. Her injuries had been dressed and she was restless with eyes shut. He bent over and whispered her name. The child opened her eyes. Certain that her parents had been lost, Zantovski said nothing of it and attempted to soothe her. He then tried to find the Datheils.

M. and Mme Datheil were already on their way to the hospital. When they arrived, they were met with the unimaginable news. The deaths of Gustave and Marjorie were confirmed and they were called upon to identify the bodies of their friends. After that ordeal, the couple were taken to the baby's bedside. Heavily bandaged and sedated, she had lost the little finger on her badly burned left hand, and there were third degree burns on the backs of her legs. Infection had set in; they were told that in spite of surviving the crash, the baby's life was still very much in danger.

Desperate for information, the Datheils asked to speak to any survivors. The next morning, they were taken to Jean's bedside. He relayed the whole experience.

He had been fully conscious throughout the crash; it was only once he'd crawled away from the plane that the pain had overwhelmed him. When he passed out he had let go of the child, who had been found crouched under a wing of the plane, 'like a little mushroom', whispered a white-faced Madame Datheil later to her husband.

She wrote a very long and detailed letter to Mona, who suffered in suspense for several days before she was able to have it translated. She finally read the full report of what had happened, including all Jean's revelations[25]. The letter went on to include news from M. Datheil's parents and her own 20-year-old younger sister Monique, who lived in Suresnes. She copied out, word for word, a passage from her sister's letter:

> I saw Mr & Mme Lange Monday 4th on the eve of their departure. Mr Lange was very nervy and Mme Lange sad and depressed. I am certain that she had a presentiment since it appears she said to Mme Petit, 'Oh Yvonne, I don't know how this journey to this wretched country is going to turn out, I am very nervous. If anything should happen to me, say a prayer for me'.
>
> Moreover, giving her jewellery into the keeping of Mr Peter, their friend in Neuilly, she gave him, at the last moment, her wedding ring to put with the other jewellery and requested that it should be for Graham if anything should happen to her.

These words were read with indescribable pain and grief. Mona, too, had known only too well of her sister's fears for this journey, and of the care Marjorie had taken to safeguard her boys.

---

[25] Full transcript Appendix D pp.264-269

CHAPTER TWENTY-FOUR

ALL AT SEA WITH THE NEWS

Before they ran into Leith harbour, the Captain approached Graham who was off duty. Instantly he knew something was wrong. Holding a radio message in his hands, the Captain said, 'Graham, I have bad news for you. Your parents have been involved in an accident. You are to call your Aunt as soon as we get into port.'

Graham was filled with foreboding. What kind of accident? Where were they? He knew they had been waiting for weeks for a visa to go to Czechoslovakia. It must be serious.

After they had docked, the Captain put on his uniform and accompanied Graham to the nearest telephone. He gave him the number and Aunt Olive answered. 'Graham, I am sorry, I have the most awful news for you. Your parents have both been killed when their plane crashed as it landed in Prague. Your sister was with them. She has survived and is in a hospital recovering from her burns, but she is okay.'

The news hit him like a sledgehammer. He was so stunned that he barely heard his Aunt's next words. 'I know this will be very hard on you, Graham, but your mother thought very highly of you. Now you must be strong and take responsibility for your brother and your little sister. They need you. Come to us now and we'll see what to do next.'

The Captain was very supportive. 'We'll go to the railway station and see when the next train goes to London. The signing off formalities can be done quickly. You'll receive your pay and you can leave tonight.'

He had six hours before the night express left from Edinburgh to London. Graham returned to the ship and in no time had packed his few belongings. As he sat on the edge at the bow of the ship and stared at the water, the pain gripped his heart. One of the men came by and asked what had happened. Upon hearing the news, he nodded. 'Aye, lad. That's the sting o' death!'

Graham said his goodbyes to all of them, thanking them for having been good comrades. He felt particularly sad to be leaving the Captain. 'Lad,' said the older man, 'It's no good arguing with your fate. You have to accept it and make the best of it. You'll come out on top and be the stronger for it. So all the best!'

On the train and alone in the carriage, the tears finally got the better of Graham. Why? Why did this have to happen after all they had been through? The war was behind them at last. The baby was still so small. We all still need them. What will it be like for Jimmy, he's only twelve? Now you'll have to face life on your own. Nobody to help you on to your feet.

Subconsciously, Graham had always hoped his parents would help him to find the opportunity to prove himself. Now the future seemed a big black hole. But as Aunt Olive had said, now he had a responsibility towards his siblings. He knew he must keep going.

Although he had shared many a good laugh with Aunt Olive, she did not exude warmth when Graham arrived. However, she did offer him some comfort, promising that he could stay with her until he could travel to Prague to fetch his sister. She had talked to her sister Mona who was prepared to take the baby and give her a good education. Anyway, Grandpa would certainly do his best to see that everything was taken care of.

Soon afterwards he travelled on to Severn Beach. Grandma received him in tears and hugged him for the first time. Graham felt like a little boy again in her arms. Grandpa told him that he had news from a person in Prague who visited his little sister – she was doing fine. She was out of danger. The doctor thought she would be able to leave the hospital in one more week and then she would have to come in as an outpatient.

The Langes' neighbour, Madame Bert Datheil had been a teacher at the French Lycee in Paris. She assured Graham that she and her husband would be happy to look after the baby and bring her into the hospital whenever necessary.

It was decided that Uncle Terry, who was a favourite among Mother's brothers and spoke French, should go with Graham to Prague as soon as they could obtain visas. When these eventually arrived on 18th May they were offered free tickets by the French Airline. By this time, the child was not only out of hospital but had completed her treatment as an outpatient. Gustave's sister, Aunt Mariechen, and her husband had collected her from the French couple and brought her to Maffersdorf.

In Prague, Terry & Graham visited the Datheils first, only to hear that his sister was no longer with them. They spoke very emotionally about witnessing the accident on

March 5th. 'All those who were meeting passengers were on the airfield and were horrified to see the plane burst into flames as it crashed. They rushed to the plane to see if they could help. It was appalling that no fire engine came until it was much too late, inexplicable since the plane had circled for twenty minutes in order to use up most of its fuel.'

They explained that suddenly they had seen a bundle fall out of the burning wreck of the fuselage and roll under a wing. In spite of the intense heat, they immediately ran to see what it was. 'There was a crying baby inside. It was her!'

They had rescued the baby and accompanied her to the hospital in a waiting ambulance. Her burns were dressed and the French couple were told that she was out of danger. The burns would heal, although they did have to amputate her little finger. They visited the child every day and rejoiced to watch her recover so quickly. 'She was so brave,' they told Graham, 'and always bright. We just fell in love with her'. They also told of their conversation with the only other survivor, the Frenchman with a Dutch name who had saved the baby's life: Jean Van der Creeden[26].

Graham and Terry then travelled the 100 kilometres north to Vratislavice, near Liberec[27]. Graham later recalled, 'What a joy it was to be able to give my little sister a big hug and to see her looking so well. Of course she didn't know me. It was my 18th birthday: 21st May, 1946'. He quickly realised that it was going to be difficult to get Aunt Mariechen to part with his sister; the whole family had become so attached.

---

[26] Correct name discovered later: Van der Veecken
[27] Post-war new names for Maffersdorf & Reichenberg

Terry impressed on them that Marjorie had had a strong premonition that she and Gustave would not return from this trip to Czechoslovakia. 'She was no doubt thinking of the unstable political situation,' he explained, 'but she has asked two of her sisters to take care of the children if something happened to them. She expressed her wish that her daughter should be brought up in England by her family. Her Grandfather has sent Graham and me to tell you this and to bring his sister back to England.'

Still reluctant, Mariechen's family felt that the baby should not leave with total strangers. They suggested Graham stay a little longer so that his sister could get to know him. When Terry left on 4th June, Graham stayed on.

Graham also wanted his sister to be in England. He anticipated that once he married he would be able to care for her himself. He continued to try to persuade his aunt that their own situation was much too precarious. She knew that all Germans had been expelled from Czechoslovakia and she and her family had been spared with help from Gustave. There was a bitter hatred of everything German and the German language was banned. This was retaliation for the welcome given to Hitler in 1938 by the Sudeten Germans. The only reason that his aunt and her husband had been allowed to stay was because his uncle was known to be anti-Nazi and he spoke perfect Czech. Gustave had written a letter from Paris to the authorities to support their case. Nonetheless, Graham couldn't countenance the idea of the baby remaining in such an unstable country.

Eventually he convinced them that the baby would be safer and have a better future in England. Very reluctantly they agreed to let her go. On 10th July 1946,

Graham and his sister were seen off from Ruzyne Airport, Prague by their cousin Liesl, the Datheils and officials of the Czech national airline, Ceskoslovenska Aerolinie CSA.

Premysl Zantovki, M. Bert-Datheil, Sylvie, Liesl and Graham

Graham was apprehensive as to how his sister would react to being on an aircraft again. Although she cried at first, she was soon distracted by some toys. For him, the experience was surreal. As he strapped himself in to his seat he held his little sister very tightly, heart pounding and mind running wild with thoughts of their parents. He felt sick but knew he must retain his composure for his sister's sake. He was astonished at how calm the baby seemed; she appeared to have no fear at all. Graham was hugely relieved when the plane landed safely and they got through passport formalities without any problem, especially as there were no papers for his sister.

They took the train from London to Bristol where Terry lived, staying with them overnight. Graham stayed long enough the next day to see his sister settled then moved on to Severn Beach, where he reported everything to Grandpa. His grandfather was very glad that Graham had managed everything so well, telling him that he hoped it would prove the best thing for the little one.

Graham left Severn Beach with mixed feelings – relief, certainly, but also a sense of foreboding. Now he must think of himself and his brother. On the train back to Southampton his mind wandered back to his parents. He had so wanted to make them proud of him. Graham had dreamed often of the day they would all be together again in England; he would show them the things he had learned, introduce them to new friends he had met. Now those hopes and dreams must be buried along with his memories.

As he boarded the train for Southampton Graham felt utterly alone. He need not have worried. A long, full and happy life awaited him.

**I know the plans I have for you,
plans to prosper you and not to harm you;
plans to give you hope and a future**

Jeremiah 29:11

THE END

AFTERWORD

The Author's Voice

So here I am, Sylvie: the child who survived the plane crash. This is my story. My story of the parents who died before I could know them. At the age of one year, six months and thirteen days I lost them, too young to recall the sound of their voices, their laughter, the warmth of their love, their goodnight kiss and the enthusiasm naturally bestowed upon a child born of a sweet reunion.

Neither, of course, can I recall their torment brought about from years of forced separation, nor the scars of their individual experiences in war torn Europe during that time. I am grateful for that, but my gratitude pales beside my sense of loss for those things I was denied of them.

Uncle Terry's job with Rolls Royce took him and his little family to Hucknall in Nottingham. For a while I was with them, and many of his subsequent letters show that he and his wife Connie had every intention to adopt me so that I could be a sister for their own newborn daughter Ann. But then there came the opportunity for them to make a new life in Canada. So my grandparents decided they wanted to be able to keep a watchful eye on me so I was sent to live with Beryl, Marjorie's youngest sister in Severn Beach, who immediately became *Mum*.

Thanks to Beryl, I did experience a mother's love in every sense and her love will never be underestimated and will always be reciprocated. When she and her husband Bill took me into their home, she had three children of her own. In those days of rationing and austerity which followed immediately after the war, it was indeed a courageous decision to take on another two-year-old. Beryl's baby girl, Dorothy (Dee), was just six months younger than me, so we grew up as sisters. Always dressed alike, we were many times mistaken for twins; Dee remains a much-loved sister to this day.

Dee, Sylvie, Graham and James, 1951

In the meantime, James was still with Aunt Liz, Grandpa's sister in Southampton, where Marjorie had left him for the time that we would be in Czechoslovakia. Graham felt the best thing for James was for him to go to a school like St Nicholas, the Catholic Boarding school he had attended near Paris and which had made such a lasting impression on him. He made enquiries at St Mary's College, a Jesuit school in Southampton.

Although not a boarding school, they took him as a single boarder straight away whilst recommending him for the longer term to a 'brother' boarding school in Shropshire. The Southampton Education Board was also very helpful; after the formalities had been settled, James was enrolled at St. Joseph's College in Market Drayton and was helped over his grief by the Jesuit Brethren there.

Once his siblings were in good hands, Graham spent many months dealing with the airlines over the compensation claim for the loss of our parents. This meant another return to Czechoslovakia the following year when compensation was paid. He also worked tirelessly to realise an investment our parents had made in some land in Riva Bella, where Marjorie had enjoyed running the guest house during that last summer before the war. It took fifteen years to finalise the sale of the land with very little proceeds, but the compensation received from the airline was used for the maintenance and education of James and myself.

At one point, Graham hit a very low spot and came close to suicide. However, a chance encounter with a young man whilst looking in the window of his favourite camera shop rescued him from the depths of despair. The young man took him home to meet his parents. His father, a Baptist pastor, and his wife welcomed Graham into their house and treated him with such kindness that there, he committed his life to the Lord Jesus Christ and to full time Christian service. He married their daughter Jayne, and the union took them to Austria with the International Mission to Miners. There they made their lives with their three children, first in the church they built with villagers in Amplwang, then through study at the Theological Seminary in Ruchlikon, Switzerland, he became a Pastor in Graz. During that time Jayne tragically died of cancer in her early forties.

His second marriage to Erika, who had been widowed at the same time, brought with it two more children, Ruth and Andreas. Graham was later transferred to the Baptist Church in Salzburg where Elizabeth and Samuel were born. He served there as Pastor until his retirement, although he continued to play an active and demanding role in the church, working with refugees until his early eighties. He was honoured by the city of Salzburg for his contribution to human rights.

James was served very well by Graham's choice of school. He fitted in well, made lifelong friends and generally excelled. After his final exams he stayed on and joined the monastery for a year before realising that his real desire was for family life.

After marrying Maureen, James went on to follow in our father's footsteps, being appointed European representative, not for carpets but for the perfume house Helena Rubenstein – based for some years in Paris, Frankfurt and Stockholm before returning to their beloved country home, High Barn in Somerset, where they raised their four children. He later became Managing Director for Christian Dior in London.

Perhaps it was because my parents were never discussed in my childhood that I felt compelled to give this account of their lives. In a generation where children were to be seen and not heard, it was a mystery to me why two other brothers would appear from time to time, who belonged to me but to no-one else in the family as brothers. Whether by some experience or just intuition, I felt very early on that these were questions best not asked.

It was probably James who, quite unwittingly, led me to this search. He had been orphaned at the age of 12; the reality of this only dawned on me when my own children reached the same age.

Not just once but four times over, I gradually came to understand just a little of the grief and shock which that sudden void would have caused. Certainly, his success both in his choice of bride and his achievements as a business leader were of his own making – but it seemed almost to serve as compensation.

Partly, I sensed that God was always on his side, but also that our mother and father were still keeping a watchful encouraging eye, prodding relentlessly at his guardian angel.

James's was by far the worst sense of loss. With him, talk of our parents conjured a preference for silence, yet his children and mine wanted so much to know more about them.

I have always tremendously admired and to some extent envied my brothers. They were multi-lingual, much travelled and worldly, accomplished in so many respects whereas I felt myself to be just a homely village girl.

Yes, I achieved more in my business career than I ever thought possible, and was blessed with a wonderful husband and four children. We spent more than nine happy years in Africa, but I still couldn't quieten the feeling that I'd been denied my background.

But now I near the end of my life, I value even more the benevolence, goodwill and love bestowed on me in my early years by the only Mum I knew, and all my family at Severn Beach.

A Tribute to *The Beach*

My earliest memories are of Sunday afternoons when the family would congregate at Grandma and Grandpa's who lived on Beach Avenue just across the road from Uncle Harry and Auntie Dorothy. Next door to them lived Uncle Bill and Auntie Bess at the junction with Osborne Road (where we lived) and where the young cousins would gather when the daily instruction came to "go out and play". Uncle Jack and Auntie Gwen, who used to live a few doors down from us, had moved to the suburbs. All three uncles were 'important people' at the Smelting Works in Avonmouth, and the fact that Uncle Jack had moved upmarket was to be reflected some years later in a gold medal posthumously awarded to him by the Royal Society for his contribution to Science. The most unassuming man who left school at 14, he was regarded by all his colleagues as a genius who devoted most of his working life to the development of the Imperial Smelting Furnace on which he held no less than 52 patents. It was ironic that I would begin my own working life in the same company and would later follow his invention halfway around the world to Zambia.

Grandpa had a car which he didn't ever drive. The uncles would sometimes drive him and James all the way to Southampton to watch his favourite Saints playing football. But on Sundays they would drive him to the pub for a drink and the aunties would gossip about things we children weren't allowed to hear. We would be allowed indoors for a short time for tea which comprised of bread and butter, beautifully sliced by Auntie Gwen who seemed especially skilled at buttering the cut end of the loaf and then producing this perfect specimen which just melted in the mouth. No jam or other accompaniments were necessary. If we were very good we'd have a bowl of fruit and jelly. On rainy days, the children would be consigned to the front room with an old biscuit tin full of photographs. It was always guaranteed to keep us amused for hours and there I would get an occasional glimpse of Marjorie with the two boys on the beach. Cousin Jacqueline seemed to know the whole story and it was she who enlightened me to my circumstance – long before I was properly told. But these were just some of our very large family who lived within a stone's throw of each other.

Severn Beach is a dot on the map close to Avonmouth. A village on the banks of the Severn Estuary, in its heyday it served as a Sunday out for trippers from Bristol who in high season poured out of the railway station in droves. It was also popular with Midlanders, who returned year after year for their summer holidays to one of the many chalets which lined the grassy area along the sea wall. Much of the housing stock and most of the main visitor attractions were owned by the landlord, Robert Stride. Revered as the local squire, his own home which he shared with his wife José was no manor house. Just a hundred yards or so from the Derhams' home which mirrored all the bungalows along Beach Avenue, it differed only from the rest in that it boasted two bay windows instead of the customary one, though it did have a rather larger garden. Later on, they moved into a purpose built two storey house in a prime position much more suited to their status.

At the river end of the avenue, alongside Mr Teacle's Putting Green, there was a pretty rose arbour leading up the steps to the sea wall and the entrance to the Blue Lagoon, an open air swimming pool which filtered its water from the Severn. From there visitors could walk past an assortment of kiosks which sold ice creams, candy floss and other seaside paraphernalia, to a variety of fairground amusements owned by Mr and Mrs Shufflebotham. Mr Shufflebotham had another very important part time job. He drove a veteran Hanson Cab as chauffeur to Barney & Joy, who claimed to be the fattest married couple in the world; a valid claim I've little doubt, because for some reason Auntie Bessie once had the job of washing Joy's bloomers which were *joyfully* huge and kept us children in stitches as they billowed on the washing line.

Of Barney, the Bristol Evening Post once reported he took a trip on the Queen Elizabeth and had to be hoisted aboard by crane because he was too fat to walk up the gang plank! (Unsurprisingly, neither Barney nor Joy lived into old age).

In the other direction, there was a mile walk along the sea wall past the small boating lake called Lakelands, on to the Pumping Station, past the old railway cottages at the foot of the Severn Tunnel and on to the New Passage Hotel. There, on weekly jazz nights, the 'in' crowd from Bristol would congregate to hear an assortment of trad bands but always, at her piano, Molly Bracey and her cigarette holder would be the main attraction. Her *cut glass* spoken English was peppered with expletives which added to the entertainment.

Fellow pupils at St Ursula's, our school in Clifton, took pity on us for living at Severn Beach but I thought it was the most wonderful place. My first school had been a private school run by Granny Poole at her house in Beach Avenue. There, I learned to read and write and dance to 'Music While You Work' along with cousin José, sister Dee (whom I later discovered was also my cousin) and about a dozen others. In fact, it was during a session on the latter that I vividly remember the announcement 'The King is dead' and, with great solemnity, school closed for the day. But on happier, more normal days Granny Poole would read us Wind in the Willows and take us to Lakelands for a nature study, where we would all be charged with searching for Ratty. I have happy memories of summer walks near Lakelands with James and Dee and Spud the dog and of Graham taking a photograph of us all on a haystack.

We would spend our Saturday sixpence watching Old Mother Reilly at the Rustic Cinema run by Mr Shufflebotham Senior, who would regularly stop the film to give the boys a sharp rebuke when they became unruly. And the next day we would all be dressed in our best clothes for Sunday School in the little tin church in Ableton Lane.

One Sunday was different from the rest, significant to my grandparents because it was their golden wedding day and significant to me because so many more of our family were there. Auntie Olive from Southampton, Auntie Flora from Swansea and Auntie Mona and her husband from Puckeridge. Auntie Mona stood out from the others by her very loud voice and mannerisms which made us children giggle. It was years later that I was to learn her extraordinary presence was the result of stone deafness which had beset her in her early twenties. Years later still, I discovered this to have been the first contact she'd had with the rest of the family since the trauma which followed the crash, by then seven years ago.

This was a very special day indeed, because we children (of which there were many) were allowed inside the house. Grandpa's billiard table was disguised as a party table and we all had a place around it with the grownups. It was a double celebration, their golden wedding coinciding with his retirement as a foreman boilermaker at the age of seventy-two. A silver table lighter presented to him by the Port of Bristol Authority received glowing admiration from all in attendance. My memory of this event is completely overshadowed by the circulation of a cheque made out in his name for the princely sum of one hundred pounds – the proceeds of a collection from of his fellow workmates – which to my astonishment received a kiss from all who touched it. Even the children joined in with the worship of this promissory note, which spelt a fortune to its proud recipient in those days.

I didn't see Auntie Mona again until just before my wedding day nearly ten years later, and quite soon afterwards I found myself the target of an unusually high measure of attention and friendliness from her. One of a multitude of nieces, I was puzzled by the overtures I alone was receiving from an aunt whom I'd met only twice in my life. And then, over a cup of tea, she told me. As if she'd saved this news for the moment, it all came out. With a mixture of sadness, bitterness and hurt resignation, she explained in her inimitable fashion how she had been my mother's closest sister and that it had been Marjorie's stated wish that she, Mona, should be my guardian in the event that anything happened to both her and Gustave. Indeed, she was adamant she'd even had the letter to prove it. It was she who had received the full account from Mme. Datheil who had been at the airport with her husband to meet us and seen the tragedy unfold with their own eyes. It was she with whom Marjorie had been in close correspondence in the final months before the accident. It was she who had given Graham a home when he arrived in England at the end of the war. She took the evidence with her to my grandparents to stake her claim and apparently the letter made a completely unexplained disappearance. Mona recalled a subsequent letter written to her by Grandpa explaining why she was unsuitable and why it had been decided that Beryl should have me.

Even then, I could understand my grandparents' decision and they will have made it with my best interests at heart; not least that I would be living in close proximity to them. But also, Beryl, my mother's youngest sister, was a plump and jolly *natural Mum*. Beryl's greatest joy was to be in the kitchen making oxtail stews and pickles. She was a good mother and I loved her dearly. She had two older sons, John and dear Colin[28], as well as Dee so close to me in age that we could be brought up as sisters within the close shelter of the Beach family. Hence, regardless of their twilight years, my grandparents would be able to keep a watchful eye on my progress and I would be able to see James when he came home for his school holidays. Mona, on the other hand, lived in Hertfordshire, many miles away from Severn Beach.

First Source of Discovery

Formidable though she was, my heart went out to Mona. Nature had determined she would have an only child, a son, and I would have been a well-timed and ready-made sister for him. Having seen the correspondence between them, I do believe she was my mother's choice and could

---

[28] Colin Dawkins went on to become a celebrated furniture maker, chosen to make the Bardic Chair for the Welsh National Eisteddfod held in Aberavon in 1966 and later, the chairs for the Queen's opening of the Welsh National Assembly in 1999.

well understand her sense of denial. I resolved immediately to try and make up for the years she'd lost of me. We kept in touch throughout the decade we spent in Africa and on our return I found myself caring for her in her old age as a daughter would. My reward was to hear, at every opportunity, her reminiscences of my mother from schooldays to the point of leaving home. Minute little snippets about her introduction to the stage and the world of dance gave me something to build on. In later years, Mona would sometimes pick up on articles in the Observer about Diaghelev, the birth of Sadlers Wells or the Blue Belles, all of which came into their own at about the time my mother left for France. And so I would speculate about whether she may have been a serious ballet dancer or perhaps a Blue Belle at the Moulin Rouge. I've since established that the Blue Belles were founded in 1932, but I'd already concluded that both notions were probably far too ambitious – although tall, she would not have qualified in height for the latter and lack of funds would have denied her proper training for the former.

Mona, who you will remember had been deaf for many years, talked very loudly and incessantly. She would often tell me about the time she visited the Guest House Marjorie ran at Riva Bella in Normandy before the war and about the great homecoming visit Marjorie made with me and James when it was all over.

Sometimes she would refer to 'one or two' letters from my mother which she would give me one day, but the years went by and I didn't doubt she'd find the right moment sooner or later.

Rena, Auntie Olive's daughter, was also a dear friend to Mona. She lived only fifteen minutes away (compared to my two hours) and often dropped in to see her for a chat. One morning an urgent phone call came through to my office from Rena, very concerned that a strange voice had answered Mona's telephone that morning. Oh, it was Mona alright, but instead of the usual 'sonic boom', she had answered with a soft, sweet faltering manner; what was more, she seemed quite oblivious to the change. Something was seriously wrong. I rang her immediately and was met with the same out of character response.

Within hours she was in hospital and a minor stroke was diagnosed, from which she recovered in part. Although she was now in her late seventies, thankfully her judgement was not impaired and she soon accepted she would have to give up her flat and her doctor recommended a nursing home. She asked me if I would clear the flat in order that it could be sold.

Among the many boxes of papers I brought home to sort out, I found them. Not one or two but probably a dozen or more letters from my mother and one from my father, the one from Grandpa and another mysterious wedge of foolscap covered in very fine handwriting and signed by Mme Bert-Patheil[29]. I didn't read them there and then, as if afraid of what they would reveal. Instead I savoured the thought for a day or two and then asked my daughter Maria (then 18) to share the moment with me. The moment turned into a very moving two or three hours as, piece by piece, the box gave up its treasure and we read aloud the words written in such anguish so many years before. In tear-filled interludes we comforted each other, cried on each other's shoulders and asked again and again, 'Why did I have to wait so long to read these

---

[29] *Datheil*: misspelt in translation – full text p.264-269

words?' I resolved to ask Mona this question very gently the following day.

The next morning, I had a serious fall and ended up on crutches. I worried about my promised visit to the Nursing Home – needlessly, as it turned out. A phone call came from Mona's son Raymond to say she had passed away peacefully with heart failure. It was a shock and I knew I would miss her badly, but for her it would have been a welcome release.

I never did get to ask her why.

Back to my Birthplace

For my fortieth birthday in September 1984, I returned to my birthplace to find my parents' final resting place with my husband and our ten year old son, Sean. It was far from plain sailing. Czechoslovakia was still in the Eastern bloc, behind the Iron Curtain. I'd been warned by the UK Home Office many years earlier that it would be dangerous for me to return. But Graham assured me that the political situation had relaxed; he had friends who had been through the border and safely returned. Nevertheless, the German surname on my passport certainly elicited hostility from the border guards, to the extent that an oil painting of great sentimental value, which we were taking to Graham as a gift from James, was seized on the outward border check on the pretext that we may have stolen one of their great works of art. In fact, the painting was one of two bought by Marjorie during their prosperous days in Paris from someone on the road who had been desperate for money.

The guards carried out a complete fingertip search of our car; we were forced to sit on the roadside in searing heat for several hours. In all, the visit was quite an adventure; despite the language difficulties I was able to find the grave, and to meet friends of my parents who remembered me as a baby. This was a great joy to me.

It was some years later that one visit to James had left me feeling in particular despair; a silly feeling that we were somehow in competition over our loss, and that mine was actually much worse than his. Of course, I was wrong but I left Maureen with the cliché, 'It's better to have loved and lost than never to have loved at all'. We both remember it in different ways but nevertheless it prompted the most amazing outcome. Her subsequent efforts have enabled me to know my parents better than I had ever thought possible.

Maureen gathered every piece of correspondence and many photographs which Graham had so carefully saved over the years. She even taped a long discussion with Graham during one of his annual visits from Salzburg. She then proceeded to piece together their lives. The result was a chronicle compiled from the love letters Gustave wrote to Marjorie in 1927, right through to the letters Marjorie sent to her sister Mona just weeks before the plane crash in 1946 and discovered by me forty years later.

The Man who saved my Life

All this research revived in me a long-held wish to trace the man named as Jean Van der Creeden who had also survived the accident. He had given a detailed account of the event and how he'd saved my life. On the fiftieth anniversary of the crash, I put out a series of press releases to the French daily newspapers. Though the exercise failed to find my hero, something else happened which was exciting. An article in a Suresnes advertiser, the local paper of a Paris suburb, was spotted by Nelly Peirani, the daughter of neighbours who had been the last to see my parents alive.

As a result of finding Nelly, Maureen and I travelled to Paris. Trips were made to the places of Marjorie and Gustave's courtship and together we visited their three homes in Paris, walking in their footsteps and through their front doors. One day we took a trip to the nearby parks and imagined Graham and Jimmy there playing children's games. We also drank coffee in a smart café in the 16th arrondissement not far from their first flat in Paris at No.3 rue Verdi, just to know how it felt. There, I was able to cast my mind back and envisage the pre-war years, their happy days in the early '30s, and Marjorie's later dreams of the *salon de thé*. I found myself so grateful for their happy years.

We had not given up on our search for Jean and eventually Maureen found his family with the help of an archivist in Suresnes. The translation that we'd had of Jean's account of the crash had spelt his name incorrectly as Van der Creeden; instead it was Van Der Veecken and, this time, we managed to locate his sister. From his family, we discovered more about Jean's background. Born in 1920 in the family's apartment in a new Paris garden suburb, he was the second child born to a half English mother and a Dutch father. Their first child, a daughter, was less than two years old and they were overjoyed to have a son.

Jean's *joie de vivre* led him into all kinds of scrapes. When sent to his room for bad behaviour, the teenage Jean would escape through the window and slide down the drainpipe, undeterred by his third floor location. He once jumped off a bridge into the Seine, but one brush with real danger was enough; that particular stunt was never repeated.

By the time the call came for military service, Jean had had a string of girlfriends but one in particular, Yvonne, had caught his eye. He enlisted with the French Air Force and was assigned to the parachute regiment. When war broke out a year later in September 1939, Jean's courage and daring soon elevated him to the Secret Service (SDECE).

Throughout the war years his family heard nothing of Jean until one evening he arrived on his mother's doorstep. He was barely recognizable with straggly, unkempt hair and a long beard, and looked as though he had not eaten for a very long time. When peace was finally declared, a clean shaven and very dashing Jean, resplendent in uniform, married Yvonne. Within just a few months of their baby's birth, he was whisked away again. Nobody knew what his assignment would be. All they knew was that he was to travel by plane to Prague; his ticket was booked for Tuesday 5th March 1946. Jean was not permitted to share details of his work, even with those closest to him.

We were able to meet Jean's niece, who with her husband took us out for a meal, and most importantly we met his widow, Yvonne. They had been divorced for some time, but we discovered that Jean owned a restaurant with a business partner and was killed in 1976 when his very fast Mercedes car crashed. She also told us that their only son had been a lorry driver and tragically lost his life when he drove his lorry in fog over the end of a dock while awaiting a ferry. She showed us a cutting of the newspaper report. Poor Yvonne had endured so much heartbreak.

My hero, Jean Van der Veecken, with Yvonne on
their wedding day, 1945

The entire visit brought me closer to my childhood and gave me a precious insight into my parents' lives. We were delighted to be able to meet Nelly and visit the apartment where she still lived, in which I'd spent my last night with my parents. She told us how clearly she remembered it all, although she had been only thirteen years old. Nelly recalled how my mother, arriving in a very anxious state, had wanted to be taken to a solicitor because she was so afraid they would not return from this trip. She removed the rings from her hand and left them in their safe custody, with her wish emphatically expressed that they should be given into Graham's safekeeping, one day for me[30]. (Ref: letter p.195)

Nelly also took me to visit her very elderly mother who was ill in hospital. She was so thrilled and talked about her old friend Marjorie and the last time they were all together under her roof.

It is unbearably poignant to know the reason that no ring was found on Marjorie. I'm not sure that she had some kind of premonition about the crash, but the fact that she dreaded the journey to Prague enough to leave her valuables behind with explicit instructions speaks volumes about how she must have felt boarding that plane. No money and no papers were found in her handbag. She had complained of her feeling of 'statelessness' – a sentiment sadly echoed in the news items we see nowadays on the plight of refugees and shared by many involved in the expulsions of the Germans from their homes in Czechoslovakia – see p.248.

---

[30] I received the jewellery from Auntie Gwen when I reached 17 and wear my mother's rings to this day

Author's Insights

As the research into my parents' lives continued, I became increasingly fascinated to find out more about their families and their younger selves. Every little piece of new information was seized upon and examined, giving me the opportunity to get to know them more than I had ever thought possible.

Legend has it that members of Marjorie's mother Lily's family were in service to Queen Victoria at Osborne House. I was interested to hear from Mona about her mother's memories of the special school she attended, provided (Mona thought) for the education of the children of those in service to Her Majesty.[31]

The contrast between the stately Osborne House and the lives begun at Rose Cottage, Osborne Road, is unmistakable. Life was hard for most families in those days; children were an integral part of a family's earning power and even if they remained at home they would be set to work supporting their mother in the interminable domestic chores. With such a large family, we know that the older girls bore a great deal of responsibility for domesticity and rearing the little ones. They certainly fled the nest – by then in Southampton – with alacrity when their chance came.

Once the older girls had left, my mother's youngest sister was protected to some extent from the hardships at home when she was farmed out to Grandpa's sister. Beryl often spoke of precocious behaviour in her cousins

---

[31] Whippingham School on the Osborne Estate in East Cowes is detailed in much of the current Osborne House literature; although it may not have been for the exclusive use of Osborne House staff, the Queen certainly took a great interest in the school's construction and its subsequent upkeep. Source: Osborne House

whilst in the custody of Aunt Liz and a requirement to perform household chores to earn her keep, but significantly there were no little ones there to look after.

Nevertheless, when things looked up and she was able to return home, Terry had started school but the last of Lily's babies, Harry, had just arrived.

Childcare may have given three of her sisters the drive to escape but it was no hardship for Beryl, who simply loved babies.

Both Beryl and Flora emerged into adulthood well trained in the domestic arts, with a heightened appreciation of family and a strong devotion to others. They were driven by duty and service. Beryl became head cook at Salisbury Teacher Training College, a first class wife and mother, and an active member of the Red Cross. She cared for her own mother (Lily) until the day she died. And she cared for me as her own daughter and became my Mum. I shall always treasure her.

Flora converted to Catholicism after marriage to her trawlerman husband, Harry. She was driven by two things: her new-found faith and the desire that her children would have the education which she had been denied. All her four children excelled, the eldest, Mon, being the first in the Derham family to graduate from university. Mon went on to commit her life as a nun in the order of the Poor Clares, first teaching in Newry and later in service to the poor, both in San Salvador and Guatemala.

Flora was also an accomplished needlewoman. Devoting many hours to the service of her church, she produced fine altar cloths and highly embellished cassocks for the priests and altar boys.

The Unmarried Mother

When I married and had four children of my own, it was an uncomfortable prospect to think of baby Graham being left with a neighbour for months on end. Of course, nowadays we correctly assign rights to children which 90 years ago would have been unheard of. Victorian families bore large numbers of children, brought up on strict morals and with rigid discipline. In my own childhood, the cane had its place in the living room for any of us who stepped out of line. It was brought into effect on many occasions for quite trivial misdemeanours – even a giggling fit at the table raised a glance in its direction.

While modern English parents might be shocked at Marjorie's decision to leave Graham, other countries, even now, have very different attitudes to their offspring.

The Filipino mother leaves her children in the care of others because of a duty to earn money abroad to provide for her parents' livelihood and the rest of the family's education.

I read recently of the small and subsequently famous son of very wealthy absent English parents in the 1950s, who was assigned his own home with full time live-in nanny and caretaker, and taken to school in his own chauffeur driven Rolls Royce. He barely ever saw his parents – such a sad tale when viewed through modern eyes.

However, even in present days this is not as unusual as we might think: I was amazed to read (in the Sunday Telegraph edition of 19th April 2015) the story of a very successful Middle Eastern entrepreneur who agreed to look after his friend's two young children as payment for staying in their absent parents' Chelsea home.

While family would normally be the first choice, Marjorie was unable to call on her siblings to take care of the baby – the older sisters had babies of their own and the youngest, Beryl, was by now carving out her own future as a cook at the Salisbury Training College[32]. Her two teenage brothers were still at home with her mother who still had two small sons to look after; we have no certainty that Marjorie had had the courage to inform her parents, anyway, until well after Graham had arrived.

There was also, of course, the shame of the unmarried mother – unbearable and inescapable in those days. As much as she missed her son, with that cloud above her head, I suspect my mother must have secretly yearned to revisit her carefree younger days.

In the late 1950s I recall the dramatic exit from our village of a friend's sister; she was banished to a convent at the age of about sixteen and never returned.

I worked at the village shop to earn a few shillings at that time and rumours were rife in the shop that she had 'got herself into trouble for living life with a capital L'.

Thankfully now such banishments are consigned to the past, but the stigma of unmarried mothers remained well into recent memory.

Certainly, and for different reasons, watching my own grandchildren grow up nowadays often brings the contrast with their great-grandparents' lives into painfully sharp focus.

---

[32] Also known as the College of Sarum St Michael 1841-1978

Expulsion of the Germans from Czechoslovakia[33]

Another event which parallels the plight of refugees in the modern world was the expulsion of the Germans from Czechoslovakia.

In the months following the end of the war, 'wild expulsions' occurred from May until August 1945. On October 28 that year, Czech president Edward Benes called for the deportation of the ethnic Germans from Czechoslovakia. The expulsions were carried out by order of local authorities, mostly by groups of armed volunteers.

Willi's daughter Margit was eighteen years old at the time. She remembers vividly the day they had to leave their home, the house that Josef Lange had built, and almost everything they owned behind. Only in the last decade of the twentieth century did the family receive a very meagre compensation for this.

Margit also recalls that the few valuables which had been entrusted to Gustave were returned years later by Liesl, when they were settled and established in West Germany.

Liesl is pictured (p.223) with Graham and me at the farewell party just before we boarded the plane back to England. She died very suddenly in her early sixties before I had the chance to meet her again. This will always be a source of great sadness to me.

The Czech government did pay for my parents' funeral. They are buried in the small village cemetery in Vratislavice, known to my family as Maffersdorf. It's a terrible irony that my mother was laid to rest, albeit with her beloved Gustave, in the place she so hated in life.

---

[33] See p.280

SS Special Concentration Camp Hinzert

Our research into Hinzert yielded some extremely disturbing facts. The SS Special Camp/Concentration Camp Hinzert was located in Rhineland-Palatinate, Germany, 30 km from the Luxembourg border.

Between 1939 and 1945, 13,600 political prisoners between the ages of 13 and 80 were imprisoned at Hinzert. Many were in transit towards larger concentration camps, where most would be killed. However, a significant number of prisoners were executed at Hinzert. The camp was administered, run and guarded mainly by the SS, who were notorious for their brutality and viciousness.

My insight into Gustave's experience at Hinzert owes much to another man's account of his own time there. Half a century later, on 9th January 1997, the Daily Telegraph[34] carried the evocative and moving story of Peter Hassall.

A phone call to the newspaper put us in touch with the British Legion, who in turn put us in touch with Peter, by then living in Canada. Considerable correspondence passed between us. Peter wrote that he had spent years researching Hinzert. A very small camp, it had been staffed by some of the worst SS elements available and, as there were so many guards, he described the prisoners' lives as though in a 'goldfish bowl' – not one movement escaped the eyes of the SS.

Consequently, prisoners were starved, beaten and worked for 18 hours a day. They would get up at 4.30am and crawl into bed at 10pm, having been relentlessly worked all day.

---

[34] See Appendix E p.270-271

On separate occasions, Graham and I have both visited the site at Hinzert. No trace of the buildings remains, but a beautiful memorial has been erected. On a large bronze plate in the memorial museum are enshrined the names, a seemingly endless list of people who were worked, starved or beaten to death there.

> "I liked sunshine, since it warmed my body, and I was hoping to be able to spend a few minutes in the sun, but Pammer had other ideas – it was time for Sunday exercises, which we had already witnessed the Sunday before from the quarantine. Nevertheless, we were totally unprepared for what came upon us. Pammer had us run around the appeal (appel) place, which was quite difficult barefoot, and, as we ran, we saw roughly twenty men and women standing on the narrow street outside the camp. They were apparently witnesses to the de-lousing process and were now watching the 'Naked Olympics'. To judge from the men's suits and the women's flower dresses, they could have been headed to church. I assumed that they considered us subhuman, for we were like skeletons and had no hair. When they turned and glued their eyes to our naked bodies, we were hardly fifty feet away from them. Then laughter broke out as Pammer ordered us to 'frog walk'. 'Lower your bottom! Jump forward! Lower your bottom! Jump forward! Quack like frogs! Jump forward! Jump higher! One assumes that frogs can jump high!' He was really pleased with himself; from time to time he glanced over his shoulder to view his audience, which included young girls who enjoyed the degrading humiliation. Finally Pammer began to get bored; he sent us to our rooms and for the first time there were no Capos who beat us on the way".
>
> Peter Hassall, British NN prisoner

One of many survivor testimonials displayed at the Hinzert Memorial Gedenkstatte SS Sonderlager/KZ Hinzert

Peter Hassall and Maurice Gould

Peter Hassall's account of the *Eingang* at Hinzert, enormously moving in its own right, was also a hugely valuable resource for me in writing this book. I am most grateful to be able to use details of his story and his suffering at Hinzert in piecing together my father's life.

Eventually, Peter sent us a short note advising us that he had accepted an invitation from the States of Jersey to attend the re-burial of his comrade. We agreed to meet him there.

On 3rd May 1997, the 55th anniversary of the boys' escape and subsequent capture by the Germans, I found myself with my sister in law Maureen at a service in St. Luke's Church at Howard Davis Park in Jersey. The occasion, finally, was a hero's burial for young Maurice.

The Governor of Jersey was there in full regalia with feathered hat. The coffin was draped in the Union Jack and borne by six young soldiers. The church was by no means full. Apart from one or two members of the press and a small number of local dignitaries, we could only see two or three members of his family. One of these was pointed out to us as Maurice's sister. By deduction, we spotted the man most likely to be Peter Hassall. After a brief introduction we agreed to meet the following morning.

At 10.30 the next day, we were greeted by the brusque, thick set man we had met the day before. He clearly did not suffer fools. Once we settled down to conversation the information just flowed.

We brought a tape recorder to that meeting which Peter was happy for us to use; much of what follows is extracted from our conversation, which became more of a monologue as it progressed.

Peter had lived with his bitterness for over half a century. It had taken a great deal of courage to overcome that and accept the invitation from Jersey's civic leaders to attend this special day.

He began by giving us the facts about the run up to war, and how he and his two friends had made grand plans to sail to the mainland with maps and charts which would help the British Army to liberate Jersey.

They had been naïve not to have realised that their coastline was one of the most treacherous in the Channel. They hit rocks before they had even left Jersey waters. One of the three drowned; the other two had to brave all the elements to get back to dry land, only to be handed in by their own people to the German authorities. In no time at all the two surviving teenagers were locked up in the Island's jail, still grieving for their friend and stunned by this betrayal.

Peter recalled how they had first been transported from Jersey to France, where they were interrogated and held by the Gestapo. It was then arranged for them to be escorted to Hinzert by the German Civilian police. They had travelled in a cell wagon attached to, of all things, the Orient Express. Their police escorts first despatched them to a prison in Trier, just up the road from Hinzert, before finally delivering them to their destination. Peter told us of the starvation, the ongoing brutality and the long days of hard labour at Hinzert. The prisoners' daily routine was breaking up stone for the construction of the autobahn, then loading it on to a horse-drawn cart. However, the absence of a horse meant that several men were required to move it instead. The cart had to be pushed, with its heavy load, for several kilometres over a number of hills. The ascent of these hills was arduous enough, but surprisingly not the worst part of the journey. The difficulty involved in preventing this man-drawn vehicle from careering out of control during descents was extreme. The ever present SS whipped and beat anyone who stepped momentarily out of line.

Peter found some comfort in the fact that many of those guards did not go unpunished. They were tried and sentenced, many to death. The notorious Commandant Paul Sporrenberg, who came just after Gustave's release, died in jail in 1957.

While Hinzert cannot be compared to such murderous camps as Auschwitz, Belsen, Dachau and Ravensbruck, its regimen was extremely strict and hundreds of prisoners there were led to their death. Because of the terrible hard work and lack of food, no one could exist there for too long unless they collaborated. It has been suggested that Hinzert was one of the cruellest camps in Germany. Peter Hassall, having spoken to many ex-political prisoners, agrees. He told us in his correspondence of his certainty that he could not have existed another six weeks under the appalling conditions.

Peter was just fifteen years of age at Hinzert. Only three years older, his companion Maurice Gould had lost fifty pounds in those six weeks. The beatings and starvation meted out to him at Hinzert precipitated his early death only a year later at the maximum security penitentiary in Wittlich on 1st October 1943.

In 1997, the year of our meeting, Peter completed his unpublished memoir: *Hitler's Night and Fog Decree or The Unknown Prisoners* held in the Jersey Archives (see bibliography p.277).

On a lighter note: Lucerne

I became so captivated by the letter written from the Hotel du Lac in Lucerne that I persuaded my husband to meet me in Zurich en route from a long spell of work in West Africa. We would catch the train to Lucerne just as my father had in October 1927. All attempts to find the Hotel du Lac were in vain, so I booked us into Grand Hotel National, which on screen so closely matched the image on the letterhead, I convinced myself it was perfectly possible that a change of ownership over the years could have prompted a change of name.

When the time came, we relaxed for a day in Zurich and excitedly set off for the station next morning. The December air hung low around the city in a damp, cold mist, but I felt confident that Lucerne was sufficiently distant for us to be able to leave the weather behind us. We really did want a clear view of the lake and the mountain, and to see the place as he'd described it. I wondered what my parents would have thought of the double decker train which we boarded in good time.

We stopped at several small stations and as each one passed I began to despair of the mist ever lifting. I was delighted when we reached daylight at the end of the very long tunnel to find the sun shining and a clear blue sky! I sent my thanks upwards.

Grand it certainly was; our room on the hotel's first floor was sumptuous. We wished we'd come the previous day and forsaken Zurich. We flung open the French doors, looked out onto the lake and breathed in the cool, fresh air with delight. To the far left was the mountain mentioned in the letter; although only its summit was visible through the clouds, hovering high enough for the scene to present itself to us with breathtaking clarity. The water provided a break in the vista. It stretched back into the distance before the buildings opposite rejoined the skyline. They snaked along to the right, as far as and beyond a bridge carrying pedestrians and traffic to our side of the lake. Most of the lakeside buildings appeared to be hotels. Statuesque and mainly nineteenth century with three or four storeys, most featured the customary terrace, now deserted because of the season. Tethered at the water's edge were a number of floating restaurants, one of which served us a simple but very pleasant lunch.

We spent the afternoon walking, not just around the lake but into the back streets where we chanced upon a fascinating exhibition of photographs, works and sketches from Picasso's later years. The photography was the work of one of his oldest friends who lived with his wife in Lucerne. This exhibition was their gift to the town.

Before supper, we set off for the hotel's cocktail lounge. Greeted by its soothing tones, I imagined my father at the grand piano where a group of locals now entertained us in song. They told us later that the Hotel du Lac had indeed been a beautiful place but had been demolished and replaced by the Post Office Building. A lovely silver haired lady promised to send me some pictures of it as it was, which she did.

The experience was, for me, a catharsis. After all the research and the discoveries unravelled of the endless struggles, the misery of war and the final tragedy, it brought me back to the positive; to young love and promise of happiness and hope. We had come full circle.

And so, in Conclusion

More than seventy years have now passed since the day of the plane crash. This book has been driven by a deep desire to know my mother and father and to tell their story. I have felt my mother's presence as I've researched her childhood, discovered her drive for independence and travel, and recognised in myself her entrepreneurial spirit. For me, their letters were a window into their souls and forged a connection with them I would never have thought possible.

I feel particularly blessed to have these tangible memories of my family. These days, it's entirely possible that a baby in my situation would have little more than emails or texts to read in later life. These usually abbreviated forms of communication cannot convey so much about the sender or evoke such a sense of time and place as the handwritten word. Of course emails also get lost – computers and gadgets don't last forever and a sheaf of printouts would be much less evocative than the huge bundle of letters I am lucky enough to have. My father's love letters to my mother have given me an insight into their strong and happy marriage. Their union survived long absences and was reinforced by their shared love of Paris and their determination to return there after the hardships of war.

I owe Graham a huge debt of gratitude for keeping all this correspondence so fastidiously. He died aged 88 in July 2016 and only weeks before his death, he gave me more letters. They had been kept so faithfully, the oldest ones written nearly ninety years ago. His letters to our mother were written with great frequency, detail and enthusiasm only three months before the crash when he started his first job as a children's tutor. Her replies to those letters have also survived, along with others written by her brother Terry from Nottingham whilst I was in his care and he was still intending to adopt me. There were also letters written by my mother to Mona before the crash, and many from Mona to Graham written after the crash. All of these letters are infinitely precious to me.

We, their children, have been looked after in many ways. Between us, we have provided our parents with 13 grandchildren, 29 great grandchildren and 6 great, great grandchildren. Of all Lily's children, Marjorie has been the most prolific. I am sure she knows it too!

I thank the Lord for each and every one of my family and for lives rich with blessings and fulfilment

Graham, Sylvie and James, Summer 2005

God holds us in the hollow of his hand,
and all shall be well,
all shall be well
and all manner of things shall be well.

Saint Julian of Norwich

Appendices

APPENDICES

A Crash details on record, *Aviation Safety Network* 261

B Official notification letter from Air France date stamped 9 March 1946 – 262

C Official list of passengers who lost their lives 263

D Translated letter from Yvonne Bert Datheil containing inside eye witness account – 264

E Daily Telegraph story 9 January 1997 270
    Transcript of above 271

F Certificate of Gustave's enrolment at the Centre of Special Engagements in the Foreign Legion on 5 September 1939 272

G Certificate of Military Service issued in Columb Bechar on 5 November, 1940, the date of Gustave's demobilisation 273

H Letter signed by Colonel Gaultier in Bel Abbès and DCRE[35] Fische dated 31May 1946 274

I Societe Francaise Radio Electrique – letter dated 6 Aug 1945 certifying Gustave's employment in Lyon from 15 April 1941to 30 January 1942 275

J Carte de Repatrie issued 15 September 1945 276

---

[35] Communal Depot of the Foreign Regiments or Dépôt Commun des Régiments Etrangers

Appendix A

AviationSafetyNetwork
an exclusive service of **Flight Safety Foundation**

FLIGHT SAFETY FOUNDATION
www.flightsafety.org

Accident description
Last updated: 19 September 2016
Status:
Date: Tuesday 5 March 1946

Type: Junkers Ju-52/3m
Operator: CSA Ceskoslovenské Aerolinie
Registration: OK-ZDN
C/n / msn:
First flight:
Crew: Fatalities: 2 / Occupants: 4
Passengers: Fatalities: 8 / Occupants: 11
Total: Fatalities: 10 / Occupants: 15
Airplane damage: Damaged beyond repair
Location: near Prague (— Czech Republic)
Phase: Approach (APR)
Nature: International Scheduled Passenger
Departure airport: Strasbourg (unknown airport), France
Destination airport: Praha-Ruzyne International Airport (PRG/LKPR), Czech Republic
Narrative:
The CSA flight to Prague (PRG) took off from Paris, France at 12:30. An intermediate stop was made at Strasbourg. The Ju-52 attempted to land twice at Prague, runway 22 and crashed on the third attempt.

Sources:

www.flightsafety.org

Appendix B

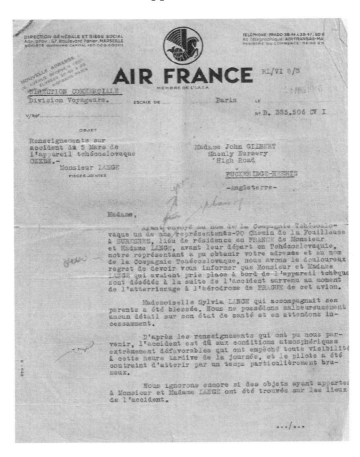

Appendix C

Official list of the passengers who lost their lives

ČESKOSLOVENSKÉ AEROLINIE
oznamují, že se rozloučí s oběťmi letecké nehody z 5. března 1946
na ruzyňském letišti, při které padlí za oběť:

Pan Karel Balík
pilot z Prahy
Pan Vladimír Parák
palubní radiotelegrafista z Prahy
Pan Vojtěch Slezák
palubní mechanik z Bystřice p. Host.
Mr. Sidney Levine
Pan Gustav Lange
Paní Margarie Lange
Pan Dr. Josef Soják
z Bratislavy
Mme. Nadia Hosanski
z Paříže
Mme. Gertrude Pinski
Mr. David Guzik
Mr. Walden

po společných smutečních obřadech v sobotu dne 9. března 1946
o 13. hod. na hřbitově v Ruzyni (konečná stan. el. dráhy č. 22).

Pohřební ústav Schönbach, Praha I

Note: Gertrude Pinski and David Guzik were among others above travelling with the Joint Distribution Committee (see p.6 and p 280: *Pinsky*)

Appendix D

Letter sent to Marjorie's sister
(Translated into English from French)

Prague 27 March 1945

My dear Madam

I owe you a long letter and this evening I am going to try and give you the details you want to know. I am so tired nowadays, I am thinking of having a few days' rest. Please do not be offended if I am a little late in writing.

First of all, news of our little Sylvie. She is getting on wonderfully. Tomorrow they will be unbandaging her left hand, the right one has already been unbandaged for eight days and our little baby is gaily using it. During the last few days Sylvie has been inoculated against scarlet fever as a child was in the ward with it a little while being isolated. This tired the child (Sylvie) and she has been off colour for three or four days but is alright now. She has no temperature and is playing and laughing. She has got used to the hospital diet. I must admit that this worried me a little as I know that Mme. Lange had not fed her like this but I asked them to give her milk and each day I take something to augment the hospital diet. All the hospital staff from the lady doctor and the doctors who are attending Sylvie, the sister, down to the maids, everyone makes a fuss of her, she is so adorable, so sweet – poor little thing.

She calls me 'Maman' and is very fond of me, I think. I am sad to think that Sylvie will disappear from my horizon. You need not worry about the little thing. I have no children but I have treated her as if she were my own.

At the same time as I received your letter. I had one from the Red Cross asking for the address of the hospital and a few details and a letter from Graham which was very moving. Never have I been so touched. At 18 years old Graham is already a man who is not afraid of the heavy responsibilities which have fallen upon him.

With regard to Sylvie, I should like you to tell me if you agree for me to keep her whilst waiting for you to take her or whether you wish her Aunt at Bratislava should have her during her convalescence. It is as you wish. You know what pleasure it would give me to keep Sylvie with me but I know that her Aunt and Mr Zantowsky also wish it. According to Graham I think he would prefer me to keep her. Will you arrange it in writing with M. or Mme Scheufler – it is a delicate question for me. I do not wish to offend anyone.

Now let us pass to the painful details which I must tell you.

I have had to identify M. & Mme Lange. Mme Lange was easily identified as there were only three ladies, an American and a young French woman. As regards Marjorie, I did not have the painful task of looking at her remains but Monsieur Lange remained with an American unidentified after 10 days and I was called upon again. I cannot tell you how painful this was for me. I reproached those responsible for the inquest for not calling upon M. Zantowsky whose address I had given and who at the time of the first identification was called by me alone.

On my insistence to the Aeroline, they decided to go to Bratislava to obtain some details which it was impossible for me to furnish. They asked me to go and I made the journey to Bratislava by car. I saw M. Zantowsky again and M. Lange's niece, Elizabeth, a very nice girl. Mme Scheufler and her husband received me in a very friendly manner and their grief upset me. I saw the flat where M. & Mme Lange had left their furniture and where they lived.

Besides my visits to Sylvie, I spend some of my time visiting a young French officer who escaped with the second pilot and another passenger, a Dr Bruno. This young Frenchman, 26 years old, was coming on business to Prague. It happens that his parents live in Suresnes garden city also, and at Rue Lafayette at the Air France Office, he had made the acquaintance of M. & Mme Lange the morning of the departure. He speaks English very well. His mother is English. His name is Jean Van der Creeden (Dutch descent). He related all this to me himself. He looked after Sylvie for a few minutes, while her parents were attending to papers and luggage. When they took their places in the plane, Mme. Lange occupied a seat **in front,** behind the engineer with this gentleman by her side and M. Lange, delayed by last minute preparations could only find a place in the rear of the plane when he came on board. You know that the Czech line, Paris-Prague, amalgamated now with Air France was inaugurated on the Monday (only the day before) and that is why, in spite of bad weather, they left. At Strasbourg the weather was so bad that the pilot was advised not to continue, but it was essential to make Prague at all costs – a business proposition. In any case, the pilot was a Czech RAF who knew the route by heart. Also, he wanted to get back to re-find his family as quickly as possible.

It seems there was imprudence, the journey should never have taken place.

When the plane arrived over Prague it was night and snowing hard. For an hour, they circled round looking for the aerodrome, that is to say the airport of Prague. M.

Van der Creeden, who was a parachutist and knew all about planes, told me how anxious he was.

'I felt the accident coming', he said. The wireless was very active and he alone knew that everything was not going right with plane. I asked him if, during this hour, the passengers and, in particular, M. & Mme. Lange, were worried. He assured me 'No'! Little Sylvie was running up and down the central corridor between her Mother and Father. The aerodrome having been at last contacted and the landing strip in sight, the descent commenced and the second pilot was obliged to open the window on account of the snow, but nothing could be seen.

M. Van Der Creeden told me 'I followed anxiously this descent and was seated on the edge of my chair to see better' [this position unfortunately cost him a broken pelvis and broken leg].

The plane was approaching the landing strip when instead of taking it in the right direction it hit broadside the under-carriage smashed, the plane broke in two and the 2,000 litres of petrol on board caught fire immediately.

All the passengers accept four, that is three and Sylvie, were trapped and this is the dramatic part – M. Van der Creeden tells me he was completely conscious the whole time and no detail escaped him. Although seriously injured, he seized Sylvie from the flames and succeeded, as you can guess, by dint of superhuman effort, in dragging himself with the child out of the plane, through a hole made by the accident, the only exit by which anyone escaped. He crawled a few metres from the plane, when his pain was so intense that he lost consciousness and let go of the child. That is why Sylvie was found under a wing of the plane like a little mushroom.

M. Van der Creeden told me he saw exactly everything what happened. M. Lange was killed instantaneously but the other passengers, amongst them Mme Lange, tried to free themselves in vain – their ordeal lasted 4-5 minutes. In spite of an injured side, Mme. Lange tried to free herself it was terrible.

I thanked my compatriot to whom Sylvie owes her life. When I first wrote, I had not seen this gentleman and our suppositions were different. If you wish to write to M. Van der Creeden, I have not got the exact address of the hospital, but write to the French Consulate in Prague and he will soon get your letter.

I have received, news from my parents and my young sister Monique – 20 years old, who lives in Suresnes. I am copying literally, a passage from my sister's letter:

'I saw M. & Mme Lange Monday 4th, on the eve of their departure. M. Lange was very nervy and Mme Lange sad and depressed. I am certain that she had a presentiment since it appears she said to Mme Petit "Oh Yvonne, I don't know how this journey to this wretched country is going to turn out. I am very nervous. If anything should happen to me say a prayer for me". Moreover, giving her jewellery into the keeping of Mr Peter, their friend in Neuilly, she gave him at the last moment her wedding ring to put with the other jewellery and requested that it should be for Graham if anything should happen to her.'

I must also mention that there was no money and no papers in her handbag. Graham has asked me in his letter if Mother was carrying a paper relating to the inheritance. I have tried to gather together every detail concerning M. & Mme Lange. I wish I could write in English but though I can read your letters it would be very long and very difficult for me to write myself in English. Perhaps I shall be nominated there next year as I do not wish to stay in Czechoslovakia but I have some anxiety as to whether I shall obtain my visa from your Consulate. If ever they refuse me I would ask you later to write to your Consul in Prague and request him to give it to me. I will write to Graham soon but I have so much to do and am so tired.

I hope soon to send you some photographs of Sylvie.

With all my affectionate thoughts and will you please convey my kindest regards to your parents and nephew.

Yours very sincerely
Y. Bert. Patheil [wrongly translated from Datheil]

Appendix E

Daily Telegraph 9 January 1997

Gerald Bisson of the Royal British Legion at Howard Davis Park, the Jersey cemetery in which Maurice Gould will be laid to rest

Jersey resistance fighter's remains come home

By David Graves

Maurice Gould: secrets

THE remains of a teenage wartime resistance fighter who was captured after trying to flee Jersey with German military secrets are to be returned to the Channel Islands more than 53 years after his death.

Maurice Gould, 18, who died in a German prison in 1943 following his capture, is buried in a military cemetery near the Luxembourg border, surrounded by his enemies, including members of the SS.

But after a long campaign the man who was captured with him and in whose arms Gould died, Jersey's public services committee has agreed that the teenager's remains can be reinterred in a war cemetery in St Helier along with British and other Allied servicemen.

Gould and his friend Peter Hassall, now 70, were captured in May 1942 after attempting to escape from occupied Jersey and sail 100 miles to England in a small open boat with details of German military placements.

They were just two miles offshore when the boat sank and a third teenager with them, Denis Audrain, a non-swimmer, drowned. Gould and Hassall managed to swim back to shore where they were arrested by German troops.

The teenagers were sent to Paris, where they were questioned by the Gestapo and SS, before being moved to a concentration camp, SS Sonderlager Hinzert. The harshness of further interrogations took its toll on Gould, who died on Oct 1, 1943, shortly after being transferred to a prison at nearby Wittlich.

Mr Hassall, who had cradled his friend in his arms as he died, was later sent to other camps in Germany and sentenced to four years' hard labour. After the war he emigrated to Canada, but never forgot his friend and wrote to the Queen, successive British prime ministers and the Commonwealth War Graves Commission in an attempt to have Gould's remains reinterred in Jersey.

But he was told he needed the permission of Gould's family before the authorities would agree to his request. Eventually the Royal British Legion helped him find his friend's sister and half-brother in Britain who gave their consent for their brother's remains to be returned.

Mr Hassall said yesterday: "When someone is lucky enough to escape hell you worry desperately about those who did not survive. I still think about Maurice every day.

"I took upon it as my duty to enable him to return home. I have visited his grave in Germany and although it is tended with respect it was surrounded by German soldiers. It was not the place it should have been left.

"It will be a relief for me when he is returned to his final resting place. Jersey was the only home he knew and is where he should be."

Gerald Bisson, president of the Jersey branch of the Royal British Legion, said: "The people of Jersey fully support the return of Maurice Gould's remains to the island. He will be reburied with the respect he deserves."

Gerald Bisson of the Royal British Legion pictured at Howard Davis Park, the Jersey cemetery where we saw Maurice Gould laid to rest

Transcript of Appendix E
Daily Telegraph extract 9.1.1997

The remains of a teenage wartime resistance fighter who was captured after trying to flee Jersey with German military secrets are to be returned to the Channel Islands more than 53 years after his death.

Maurice Gould, 18, who died in a German prison in 1943 following his capture, was buried in a military cemetery near the Luxembourg border, surrounded by his enemies, including members of the SS.

Gould and his friend Peter Hassall, now 70, were captured in May 1942 after attempting to escape from occupied Jersey and sail 100 miles to England in a small open boat with details of German military placements.

They were just two miles offshore when the boat sank and a third teenager with them, Denis Audrain, a non-swimmer, drowned. Gould and Hassall managed to swim back to shore where they were arrested by German troops.

The teenagers were sent to Paris, where they were questioned by the Gestapo and SS before being moved to a concentration camp, SS Sonderlager Hinzert. The harshness of further interrogations took its toll on Gould, who died on October 1st 1943, shortly after being transferred to a prison at nearby Wittlich.

Mr Hassall, who had cradled his friend in his arms as he died, was later sent to other camps in Germany and sentenced to four years' hard labour.

But he was told he needed the permission of Gould's family before the authorities would agree to his request. Eventually the Royal British Legion helped him to find his friend's sister and half-brother in Britain who gave their consent for their brother's remains to be returned.

Mr Hassall said yesterday, 'When someone is lucky enough to escape hell you worry desperately about those who did not survive.'

Appendix F

Certificate of Gustave's enrolment at the Centre of Special Engagements in the Foreign Legion on 5th September 1939.

Appendix G

Certificate of Military Service

Issued to Gustave on 5th November 1940, the date of his de-mobilisation. Signed by Lieutenant Mutel, Commander of the 1st Company of Foreign Workers, it certifies that on 10th November 1939 Gustave presented himself for military service as a volunteer for the duration of the war and served with his unit in Colomb Béchar.

Appendix H

Record from the DCRE (Dépot Commun des Régiments Étrangers) signed by Colonel Gaultier on 31st May 1946 with Certificate of Military Service below

Appendix I

This certifies that Gustave Lange was employed by the
The Société Française Radio-Électrique in Lyon from
15 April 1941 to 30 January 1942

Appendix J

Carte de Rapatrié issued to James on 15 September 1945

Bibliography

William Wiser *The Crazy Years, Paris in the Twenties*, Thames & Hudson Ltd, 17 April, 1990

David T Zebecki *World War II in Europe – An Encyclopedia, Munich Crisis and Agreement p.118*, Routledge, 1 May 2015

PE Caquet *The Bell of Treason, The 1938 Agreement in Czechoslovakia*, Profile Books, 28 August 2018

CB Dear and MRD Foot *The Oxford Companion to World War II*, Oxford University Press, 2001

EX-Lance-Corporal-X *The SAS and LRDG Roll of Honour 1941-47*. SAS-LRDG-RoH 2016

Graham Gustave Lange: *From Shades of Night – A Life transformed by Love* privately printed, 2008

P. Hassall, *Hitler's Night and Fog Decree* or *The Unknown Prisoners* Unpublished Memoir, 1997 Jersey Archives www.frankfallaarchive.org

Above translated into German by Landeszentrale fur Politische Bildung Rheinland-Pfalz www.politische-bildung-rip.de

Publication: *The Former SS-Special Camp/Concentration Camp at Hinzert 1939-1945* Authors: Volker Schneider & Dr. Helmut Peifer. Translated into English by Susan Hubert. Landeszentrale fur Politische Bildung Rheinland-Pfalz

Primary Sources

Letters from Gustave to Marjorie, handwritten in English from 19th May 1927 to April 1929. They were sent from Paris, Lucerne, Basel-Basel, Reichenburg, Luc sur Mer, Stuttgart and one unknown

Gustave's career history and letter of his appointment to I. Ginskey – 1928

Letter from Marjorie to Elizabeth Walwyn Bennett outlining proposals for the Salon de Thé – 1937

Certificate of Gustave's Enrolment dated September 1939 issued by the **Centre of Special Engagements in the Foreign Legion** on 5th September 1939.

Centre D'engagements Speciaux a la Legion Etrangere Certificat de Presence au Corps dated 5.11.1940; also Certificate Position Militaire confirming Gustave's time served in Bel Abbas, Algeria

Several Letters (handwritten in German) from Gustave to Marjorie after his demobilisation from 24th March to 15th December 1941. The latter has an envelope bearing the mark 'opened and censored by the Gestapo"

Several Letters (handwritten in German) from Gustave to Marjorie during his internment at Hinzert 1st February 1942 and Niederbuhl dated 19th February to 4 March 1942

Telegram from Gustave dated 18th April 1942 announcing his release

Primary Sources contd.

Letter from Graham to his parents from his Anti-Aircraft Unit FLAK dated 8th September 1944

Daily Telegraph extract of Britain at War first published May 1945

Carte de Rapatrié issued to James dated July 1945

Several letters from Marjorie to Mona Gilbert written in late 1945/early 1946

Letter from Air France dated 9th March 1946

Letter from James to his parents, undated, but written in early March 1946

Derniere Nouvelles edition of Le Monde dated 7th March 1946 showing details of the crash.

Letter from Premysl Zantovsky dated 13th March 1946 to William and Lily Derham

Original handwritten translation of letter dated 27th March 1946 to Mona Gibert from Yvonne Bert Datheil

Fiche pour le D.C.R.E issued by Registere des Armees D.C.R.E signed by Colonel Gaultier on 21st May 1946

Correspondence with Peter Hassall and taped interview

Map of SS Sonderlager Hinzert highlighting Gustave Lange's 'Stube' (hut)

FOOTNOTE Sources

p.6 Joint Distribution Committee – Footnote 1
Source: *JDC Archives: in-memoriam/gertrude-pinsky/*

p.9 Karlovy Vary (Karlsbad) Film Festival – Footnote 2
Source: *"Rita Hayworth Visiting Prague" tresbohemes.com 22 October 2015*

p.43 Ginzkey/Porsche Origins – Footnote 4
Source: *Porsche Great Britain copy – Edited https://newsroom.porsche.com/en/christophorus/issue-381/porsche-christophorus-ferdinand-origins-maffersdorf-13671*

p.97 Sidi Bel Abbès – Footnote 7
Source: *Historynet.com World War II: A Tale of the French Foreign Legion*

p.119 Footnote 9 – Egon Zill Hinzert Commandant Jan. to April 1942 Source: *Publication: The Former SS-Special Camp Concentration Camp at Hinzert 1939-1945.* (see p.277)

p.121 Niederbuhl: Operation Pistol – Footnote 10 cited as the camp from where Pvte Gerhard Wertheim was assassinated by the Germans in Sept.1944
Source: *SAS and LRDG Roll of Honour 1941-47*

p.148 Dresden Footnote – Footnote 19
Source: *dresden.de/historicalcommission*

p.160 Footnote 20
Source: *Daily Telegraph, first published in May 1945 in the Daily Telegraph and Morning Post.*

p.171 Footnotes 21, 24 (p.198) and 33 (p.248)
The final agreement for the expulsion of the German Population – Potsdam Conference, 2nd August 1945

Disclaimer: I. Ginzkey

Further information has also emerged about the Ginzkey works, the source of Gustave's long and successful career. According to Graham, the Ginzkey Factory, like the Lange family home, was expropriated from the owners by the Nazis who used it for making munitions. My German cousin Margit, Willie's daughter, strongly contests this, telling me that they continued to make carpets for the Fuhrer.

Years later, after Germany had surrendered and when victory over Europe was declared, the PoWs who worked alongside Gustave in the Ginzkey factory after his release from prison camp invited our entire family to attend as guests of honour at a victory celebration meal. I have a treasured photograph of this event which included me, a baby on my mother's knee – the sole surviving image of the two of us together.

Printed in Great Britain
by Amazon